KIDS' BOOK
OF
HOCKEY

Eric Lindros and teammates celebrate. (© Jim McIsaac/BBS)

KIDS' BOOK OF HOCKEY

Skills, Strategies, Equipment, and the Rules of the Game

John Sias

A Citadel Press Book
Published by Carol Publishing Group

This book is dedicated to Terry Slater, late hockey coach of Colgate University. In his 15 years at Colgate, Terry's teams won 251 games, making him the winningest coach in that college's history. In 1990, Terry was named Coach of the Year for both the NCAA and the ECAC. Suffering a stroke on December 5, 1991, he died four days later on his fifty-fourth birthday. Terry always insisted, "Above all, I am a teacher," and it was through Terry's advice and encouragement that this book came to fruition. Hopefully, it will teach some of today's young girls and boys the basics of the sport Terry loved so much.

Copyright © 1997 John N. Sias

A Citadel Press Book
Published by Carol Publishing Group
Citadel Press is a registered trademark of Carol Communications, Inc.

Editorial, sales and distribution, and rights and permissions inquiries should be addressed to Carol Publishing Group, 120 Enterprise Avenue, Secaucus, N.J. 07094

In Canada: Canadian Manda Group, One Atlantic Avenue, Suite 105, Toronto, Ontario M6K 3E7

Carol Publishing Group books may be purchased in bulk at special discounts for sales promotion, fund-raising, or educational purposes. Special editions can be created to specifications. For details, contact Special Sales Department, Carol Publishing Group, 120 Enterprise Avenue, Secaucus, N.J. 07094.

Manufactured in the United States of America
10 9 8 7 6 5 4 3 2 1

Library of Congress Cataloging-in-Publication Data

Sias, John.
    Kids' book of hockey : skills, strategies, equipment, and the
rules of the game / by John Sias.—1st Carol Pub. ed.
        p.   cm.
    "A Citadel Press book"—T.p. verso.
    Summary: Uses a question and answer format to explain the basics
as well as finer points of this fastest of all team sports.
    ISBN 0-8065-1921-5 (pbk.)
    1. Hockey—Juvenile literature.   2. Hockey—Training—Juvenile
literature.   3. Hockey—Equipment and supplies—Juvenile literature.
4. Hockey—Rules—Juvenile literature.   [1. Hockey.]   I. Title.
GV847.25.S46   1997
796.962—dc21   97-21631
                                                                   CIP
                                                                    AC

Contents

Acknowledgments

This book has had more changes than a new baby. It takes hours and hours to carefully examine 600-plus questions and answers. Over the years, a dozen people to whom I've submitted one edition or another have critiqued, criticized, and corrected it while pointing out inconsistencies, repetitions, and things that just plain confused them.

First was Terry Slater, to whom I've dedicated this book. Then Larry Fudge, assistant athletic director at Boston University; Paul Labarre, hockey coach at a small New England college; Rich Ladew, a student at the University of New Hampshire, to whom hockey was a brand-new activity; Chris Lovergine, a sports fanatic; Chris McMullen, my little brother who decided to attend Boston U. because he liked their hockey team so much.

And Brian Durocher, an All-American goalie and college coach; John Melanson, a professional referee; Joe Peters, a player, teacher, and fan of the game; Roger Slawson, an attorney who dissected the book piece by piece; and especially Don Vaughan, the current hockey coach at Colgate on whose expertise I depended so heavily.

My thanks to these persons who, after seeing a draft of the book, still encouraged me to continue: Joe Bertagna, goaltender coach of the 1994 US Olympic team; Bill Cleary, Harvard Athletic Director; Mike Eruzione, star of the 1980

US Olympic team; Mike Milbury, former Boston Bruins star and general manager of the New York Islanders; and Bobby Orr, the NHL's greatest scoring defenseman.

And for their steadfastness in helping to bring this little book to publication, thank you Ella Stewart and Charlie Burdick.

To my wife Marie, who pulled all the pieces together after a power surge destroyed our computer with this book on it, how can I thank you enough?

John Sias
1997

Introduction

I hesitate to tell anyone how to read a book, but you could start this one by turning to the beginning and reading right to the end. But nobody's going to do that! Maybe you could look at the contents, see something that interests you, and turn to that section. Or you could just jump around. You might even make a game of it by covering the answer and seeing how close you come to guessing it. You and a friend might make a contest: you could read a question and see how close he comes to the answer. Then it's his turn.

You could even bring the book with you to a hockey game.

If you come across a term you don't understand, read on (the term is sure to be defined later) or turn to the back of the book where you'll see key terms defined.

Learn and have some fun!

"The Great One," Wayne Gretzky (© Jim Leary/BBS)

Chapter 1

SOME HOCKEY BASICS

If you're relatively new to hockey, it might be helpful to begin at the beginning and get the basics down first. You'll see many of these basics explained in greater detail later in the book.

Q. *At age ten, standing 4′ 4″, how many goals did Wayne Gretzky score while playing for the "Nadrofsky Steelers" in his hometown of Brantford, Ontario?*
A. *In 85 games, he scored 378 goals, winning the league scoring race by a margin of 238 goals. The next two highest scorers on his team had 111 and 46 goals respectively.*

What's different and unique about hockey?
1. It's the only game in which players are substituted "on the fly." This means the game continues while some players leave the ice and others take their place.
2. It's one of the few games in which each player is equipped with a stick.
3. It's the only game played on ice, with the exception of curling.
4. It's the fastest team sport, with players skating at up to 30 MPH.

5. Although indoor versions of some outdoor sports (soccer, lacrosse, and arena football) have a playing surface surrounded by vertical sides, hockey is the only major sport to do so. These vertical sides are called the "boards."
6. The playing object (the puck) is often propelled at more than 100 MPH.
7. The playing object is extremely hard, harder than a baseball.

What's the object of the game?

The object of the game is to score more goals than your opponent does.

What's a goal?

A goal is a score. It is made when the puck enters any part of the 4′ × 6′ goal. The puck must completely pass over the red line that runs across the mouth of the goal on the ice surface. (See figure 3.)

How will I know when a goal is scored?

You'll see a red light turned on behind the goal cage. And you'll hear a lot of cheering!

Is anyone on my team allowed to score a goal?

Yes, even the goalie. And anyone on your team can even (accidentally, we hope) score for the other team in *your* goal. And it counts!

How does a game begin?

The game begins with a "face-off" in the center of the rink.

What's a "face-off"?

A face-off is a procedure used to start play or to resume play. In a face-off, an official drops the puck between the sticks of two opposing players. Any player may participate in a face-off.

How big is a hockey rink?

The rink is 200 feet long and 85 feet wide. That's two-thirds the length of a football field.

What are the five circles on the ice?

These are the face-off areas that are used most often. Most face-offs take place in one of these five circles. The face-off circle in the middle of the rink is where the game starts. (See figure 4.)

What are the four small red dots in the neutral (middle) zone?

These are face-off *spots*. Face-offs occur on these spots but not as often as in the five face-off circles. The location of a face-off is determined by where on the ice the official stopped the play.

A face-off does not have to take place within a face-off circle or on a face-off spot. (See figure 4.)

The rink is divided into three zones. What are these three zones called?

They are called the attacking zone, the neutral zone, and the defending zone.

Each team has its *own* attacking zone and defending zone. (See figure 1.)

Are players restricted to a specific zone of the rink or can any player skate anywhere he wants to?

Except when offside, a player may skate on any part of the rink at any time.

When is my team called the "attacking team"?

Your team is the "attacking team" when it has possession of the puck.

When is my team called the "defending team"?

Your team is the "defending team" when it does *not* have possession of the puck; when your opponents control the puck.

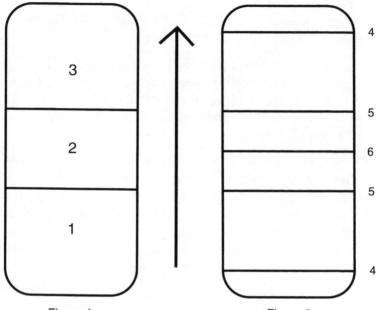

Figure 1   Figure 2

FIGURE 1.   The rink's zones. Your team is shooting in the direction of the arrow. Section 1 represents your team's Defending Zone, or your opponent's Attacking Zone. Section 2 is the Neutral Zone, while section 3 is your team's Attacking Zone, or your opponent's Defending Zone.

FIGURE 2.   The rink's lines. Number 4s are the goal lines, number 5s are the blue lines, and number 6 is the center (or red) line.

How long is a game?

A game is 60 minutes long, divided into three 20-minute periods on the game clock.

How many players are on each team?

There are 20 players, including two goalies, on each National Hockey League (NHL) team. The National Collegiate Athletic Association (NCAA) calls for 21 players, including three goalies.

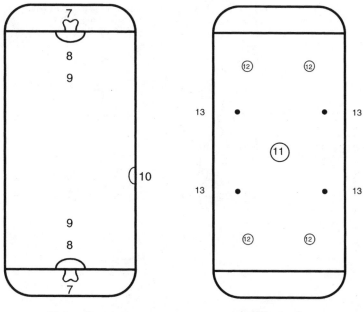

Figure 3   Figure 4

FIGURE 3.   Goals, slots, and creases. The 7s are the goals, the 8s (the light-blue semicircles in front of the goals) are the creases that the goalies patrol. The 9s represent the "slots," unmarked areas between the face-off circles in front of the goal. Number 10 is the referee's crease, a semicircle adjacent to the boards, the referee's "safe haven" where no player can enter.

FIGURE 4.   The rink's face-off circles and spots—there are nine of them. Number 11 is the center ice face-off circle; the 12s are the other major face-off circles, while the 13s represent the face-off spots.

How many players on a team can play at one time?

Six players on a team can play at one time—a goalie, two defensemen, two wings, and one center. (See figure 7.)

What is the job of each of the six players?

The goalie's job is to prevent the puck from entering his goal. The two defensemen try to prevent the other team

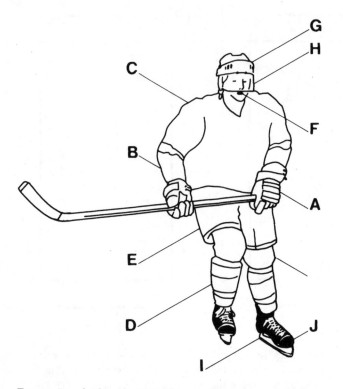

FIGURE 5.   A player's protective equipment:

(A) Gloves
(B) Elbow Pads
(C) Shoulder Pads
(D) Shin Pads
(E) Padded Pants

(F) Mouth Guard
(G) Helmet
(H) Face Guard
(I) Safety Heel Tips
(J) Hard Plastic Toe Area

from shooting at their goal. And the center and two wings are primarily offensive players who try to score goals for their team. But due to the fast action of the game, players are often required to exchange jobs instantly.

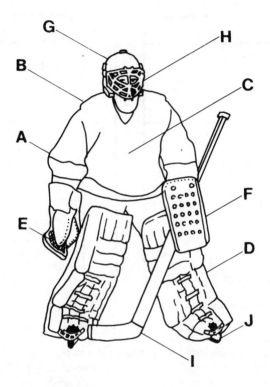

FIGURE 6. Goalie equipment:

(A) Arm Pads   (F) Blocker Mitt
(B) Shoulder Pads   (G) Helmet
(C) Chest Protector   (H) Mask
(D) Wide Leg Pads   (I) Wide Stick
(E) Trapper Mitt   (J) Padded Skates

What equipment do players use?

Each player has about 27 pounds of clothing and equipment including skates, stick, protective pants, shoulder pads, elbow pads, gloves, cup, socks, sweater, helmet, faceguard, mouthpiece, and shin pads. (See figure 5.)

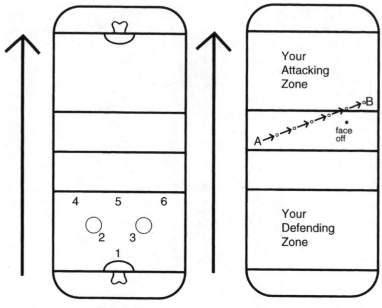

Figure 7   Figure 8

FIGURE 7.   Positions of your six players (your team is shooting in the direction of the arrow): (1) Goalie, (2) Left defenseman, (3) Right defenseman, (4) Left wing, (5) Center, (6) Right wing.

FIGURE 8.   Offside, Example 1: You're shooting in the direction of the arrow. Player A and player B are on your team. A passes the puck to B. B crosses the blue line *before* the puck does. B is offside. B is not allowed in his team's Attacking Zone until the puck is already in the zone. The official stops play, and your team loses control of the puck. A face-off will be held on the Neutral Zone face-off dot outside the Attacking Zone, or where the pass originated. No penalty will be assessed.

How many officials are there always on the ice?

There are three—one referee and two linesmen—in the National Hockey League (NHL). But in the National Collegiate Athletic Association (NCAA), there are two referees

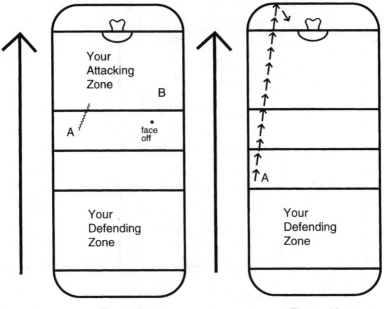

Figure 9   Figure 10

FIGURE 9.   Offside, Example 2: You're shooting in the direction of the arrow. Player A and player B are on your team. B crosses the blue line and enters his team's Attacking Zone. A is in possession of the puck. He skates across the blue line, entering his team's Attacking Zone. B is offside. He should have waited for A to cross the blue line ahead of him. The official stops play, and your team loses control of the puck. A face-off will be held on the Neutral Zone face-off dot outside the Attacking Zone, or where the pass originated, close to the blue line. No penalty will be assessed.

FIGURE 10.   Icing: You're shooting in the direction of the arrow. Player A is on your team. A shoots the puck from his half of the rink, across the center red line, across the blue line, and across the goal line. No player on either team touches the puck before it crosses the goal line. An official stops play, and your team loses control of the puck. A face-off will be held in your team's Defending Zone. No penalty will be assessed.

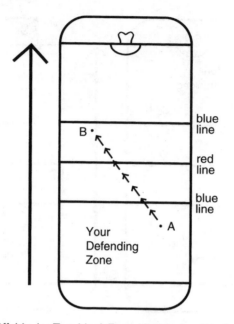

FIGURE 11.   Offside (or Two Line) Pass. You're shooting in the direction of the arrow. Player A is on your team. A passes the puck over two lines (his own blue line and the center red line). An official stops play, and your team loses control of the puck. A face-off will be held in your team's Defending Zone, just inside the blue line, in line with the face-off dot. (Note: There is no such thing as an offside pass in the NCAA.)

and one linesman. One of the referees is the "head ref" and the other is the "assistant ref." The "head ref" is responsible for calling most of the penalties, but any of the three officials *can* call a penalty.

What are usually the most difficult things for a new fan to understand about hockey?

It's usually difficult for a new fan to understand icing, offside, the offside pass, and the goalie's skating off the ice right in the middle of the game, leaving his goal wide open.

What is icing?

Icing is an illegal shot that sends the puck across the middle red line all the way to the other end of the rink and the puck crosses the goal line of the opposing team (not necessarily going to the goal). Play is stopped and a "face-off" is held in the defending zone of the team that shot the puck. Icing often happens when a team desperately tries to get the puck out of their defending zone to avoid having their opponents score a goal on them. (See figure 10.)

When is a player offside?

A player is offside when he crosses the blue line of his team's attacking zone before the puck does. (See figures 8, 9, and 12.)

What is an offside pass?

A shot that sends the puck over *both* the skater's own blue line and the center red line before it is touched by another player on his team. This occurs *only in pro hockey* (NHL), not in college (NCAA). (See figure 8.)

What's the purpose of the single red line that bisects the rink?

In pro hockey, it is an important part of the "offside pass" ruling. In college hockey, the red line has little significance other than it plays a key role in the icing rule.

What do the two blue lines mean?

First, they are an important part of the offside ruling. Second, they divide the rink into three zones—the attacking zone, the neutral zone (the middle area), and the defending zone. (See figure 2.)

Q.   *To surpass this player, a skater entering the NHL would have to average 100 points each season for 18 years, and average 52 goals a season for 15 years. What's the name of this player?*
A.   *Gordie Howe.*

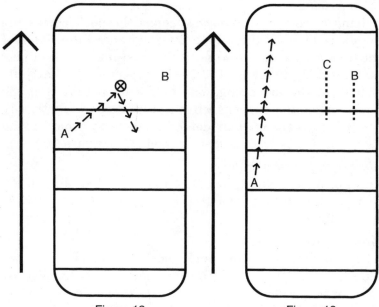

Figure 12   Figure 13

FIGURE 12.   Delayed Offside. You're shooting in the direction of the arrow. A and B are on your team. A attempts to pass the puck to B, B is offside. However, the official delays calling B offside because he sees that your team is about to lose control of the puck to player X (on your opponents' team). X passes the puck back across his own blue line and into the neutral zone. Your team has lost control of the puck, and the official does not call offside. Play continues, no penalty is assessed.

FIGURE 13.   The "Tag Up" Rule. You're shooting in the direction of the arrow. A, B, and C play for your team. A fires the puck over the blue line into your team's Attacking Zone. The official delays calling B and C offside because no player on your team has yet touched the puck. If B or C does touch the puck, they will be offside; however, if B and C both skate outside their Attacking Zone and touch the blue line (tag up), they will not be offside. As soon as they touch the blue line, they may reenter the Attacking Zone. The official will not call offside, and play continues. (The NHL eliminated this rule in 1996; it applies only in the NCAA.)

What are some common penalties?
Tripping and interference are two of the most common penalties which the officials might call against offending players.

What is the "penalty box"?
This is an area beside the ice where players are confined who have been penalized.

What happens to a player who receives a penalty?
He could be sent to the penalty box for two or five minutes depending on the particular penalty assessed against him. His team would play with one fewer player than the opposition. Or he could be ruled off the ice for ten minutes or even banished entirely from the game, in which case a substitute would play.

What is a "power play"?
That's when one team has more players on the ice than the opposing team, because of a penalty. The team with more players attempts to keep the puck inside their own attacking zone (the opponent's defending zone) until it scores a goal.

How should I watch a game?
Although the natural tendency is to watch the puck, once in a while stop watching the puck and keep your eyes on a specific player. See what he does when he does *not* have the puck. See how he gets into position to try to break up a play if the other team has possession of the puck. Or if his team has the puck, watch to see how he gets into position to receive a pass. Or keep your eyes on a team's best scorer and see what he does to put himself into position to shoot at the goal.

Should I change my seat location if I can?

Great idea. If you are able to, stand behind the goalie and see what it's like to face a puck shot right at you at 100 MPH. Or get next to the plexiglass and feel the impact of players crashing into each other. Or sit way back and watch how a play evolves from behind one goal, crosses the defending zone, sweeps into the neutral zone, and finally zooms into the attacking zone. Or sit next to the plexiglass in one of the four corners and see how the players compete against each other trying to gain control of the puck.

1980 U.S. Olympic Team captain Mike Eruzione

Chapter 2

A SHORT HISTORY OF HOCKEY

What's America's fastest-growing major sport? Hockey, of course!

Q. *In 1909, how much did mining magnate Ambrose O'Brien pay Cyclone Taylor to play for his team in Renfrew, Ontario?*
A. *$5,000. On a per game basis, the $400 per game rate Taylor received was ten times the rate paid to Ty Cobb, baseball's greatest star of that era.*

THE EARLY DAYS

How did "hockey" get its name?

In 1740, French explorers of the St. Lawrence River valley came upon a group of Indians playing a game on the ice that was similar to lacrosse. They observed, legend has it, that whenever an Indian player was hit on his unprotected body by one of the curved sticks, he cried out, "Ho-Gee!"

Why is Kingston, Ontario, recognized as the site of the first "organized" hockey game?

In 1867, the Royal Canadian Rifles, stationed at Tête-du-Pont barracks, one cold winter morning shoveled the snow off a section of Kingston Harbor and played a game of "hockey."

When was the first hockey game played with "modified rules"?
The first game was probably played on March 3, 1875, in Montreal when McGill University students adapted lacrosse rules to a new game played on the ice at the Victoria Skating Rink.

Who published the first set of rules?
W. F. Robertson and R. F. Smith of McGill University in 1879.

When was the first game played in the US?
Yale played Johns Hopkins in New Haven in 1893.

What was the first genuinely professional hockey team?
The Portage Lakers of Houghton, Michigan, organized in 1902.

What was the first professional hockey league?
The International Professional Hockey League, organized by Dr. J. L. Gibson, a dental surgeon from Ontario. Teams were from Portage Lake, Calumet, Pittsburgh, and Sault St. Marie, Michigan.

When was the first international college game?
In 1906, Harvard played McGill, a game which the latter won easily.

For years, a hockey team was comprised of seven players. When was the six-man team adopted and whose idea was it?
William Northey of the Montreal Arena is credited with the six-player concept, which was adopted in 1911.

When was the first artificial ice rink built?
In 1912, the Patrick brothers, Frank and Lester, constructed two artificial ice rinks in Vancouver and Victoria, British Columbia.

How did the NHL get its start?
In 1916, there were six teams in the now defunct National Hockey Association. When bitter feelings erupted

between the owner of the Toronto club and the owners of the other five clubs, the five owners dissolved the NHA. This left the Toronto owner on the outside, in possession of a team but with no league in which to play. To complete the "execution" of the Toronto owner, these five owners formed the National Hockey League (NHL)—without the Toronto owner, of course.

When was the NHL (National Hockey League) organized?
    In 1917.

Who were hockey's greatest innovators and what were some of the things they introduced to the professional game?
    The Patrick brothers, Lester and Frank, working from 1912 to 1925, placed a number on each player's jersey, instituted the blue lines, began the recording of assists, initiated the penalty shot, developed the league playoff system, and brought American teams into their league, the Pacific Coast League.
    They also changed the rules to allow a goalie to sprawl on the ice. Up to that time, the goalie was required to remain upright, on his skates, at all times.

Where was hockey's first Hall of Fame?
    In Kingston, Ontario.

Why did a bell replace the referee's whistle on outdoor rinks?
    When the ref blew his frozen whistle, it often violently removed the skin from his lips.

1920 TO 1980

What did King Clancy do to win, almost singlehandedly, the Stanley Cup for Ottawa on March 31, 1923?
    During the course of the game, he played all six positions in a 1–0 victory.

Which team was the first US-based franchise in the NHL?
The Boston Bruins were the first US-based franchise in the NHL. They played their first game on December 1, 1924, beating the Montreal Canadiens 2–1.

When was the first All-Star game played and how did it come about?
Ace Bailey, a popular player for Quebec, was severely injured in a collision with Eddie Shore of the Bruins. An "Ace Bailey Benefit" was organized. In the February 1934 benefit game, the Toronto Maple Leafs played an all-star team comprised of players from the other teams in the league.

When was the first NHL All-Star team selected?
In the 1930–31 season.

What American-born major league baseball umpire coached a Stanley Cup winner?
Bill Stewart, a National League umpire, led the Chicago Blackhawks to the Cup in 1938.

Which two major changes in the rules took place during World War II?
The sudden-death overtime was abolished, except for playoff games, and the center red line was adopted.

What was the name of the first full-blooded native Canadian player to play professionally?
Fred Saskamoose. He played for the Chicago Blackhawks in 1954.

Which was the first team to travel regularly by air rather than by train?
The Boston Bruins in 1958 adopted air travel. Most other teams soon followed suit.

Before its gold-medal victory in the 1980 Olympics, when had the US hockey team last won a gold?
In 1960.

1980s TO NOW

What has spurred the greater interest in American hockey?

The popularity of hockey in the last few years is due primarily to the new NHL teams in Florida and California, and to the broadcasting of more hockey games on TV. In the early 1980s, there was a renewed interest in hockey which can be attributed to the US Olympic team's against-all-odds gold-medal win, taking the crown from "arch-enemy" team Russia.

How many members of the 1980 US Olympic team joined the NHL?

Thirteen players from the gold-medal-winning 1980 US Olympics team played in the NHL. Eight went pro the year after the Olympics, the others played in Europe first or went back to college before turning pro. The Olympic players who went pro are: Goalie Jim Craig; Defensemen Bill Baker, Dave Christian, Ken Morrow, Jack O'Callahan, and Mike Ramsey; Centers Neal Broten, Mark Johnson, Mark Pavelich, and Mark Wells; Left Wing Rob McClanahan; and Right Wings Steve Christoff and Dave Silk.

Who was the first American collegiate coach to be signed to coach a NHL team?

The Calgary Flames signed Bob Johnson, a coach at the University of Wisconsin, to be their coach in 1982.

Who was the first American high school boy to jump directly into the NHL?

Bobby Carpenter, an 18-year-old from Peabody, Massachusetts, was signed by the Washington Capitals to a three-year contract for $600,000 in 1981.

How well did he do in his first year in the NHL?

In 1981–82, Bobby played in all 80 games, scoring 32 goals and 35 assists. He was the first American to score 50 goals in one season.

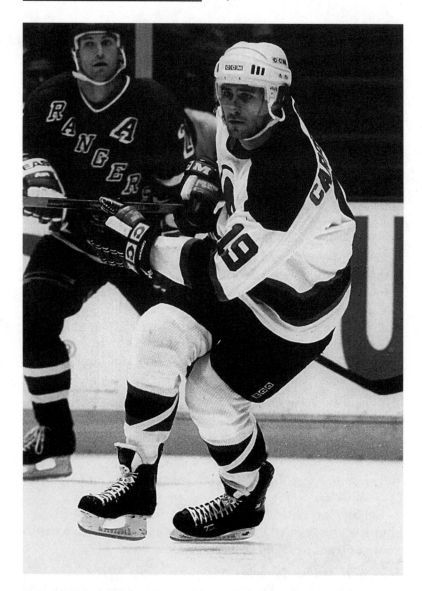

Bobby Carpenter, the first American to go to the NHL directly from high school. (© Jim Leary/BBS)

Which was the first US-based NHL team to win four consecutive Stanley Cups?
The New York Islanders, in 1979–82.

In its seven-year existence, how many teams played in the former WHA (World Hockey Assn.)?
Twenty-eight different teams.

Who have been the six league presidents since the NHL began in 1917?

1. Frank Calder   1917–43
2. Red Dutton   1943–46
3. Clarence Campbell   1946–77
4. John Ziegler   1977–92
5. Gilbert Stein   1992–93
6. Gary Bettman   1993–

Chapter 3
RULES

Why did the ref blow his whistle? Why did he stop play? Hey, what's going on out there?!

Q. *John Wensink was an "enforcer" (also called a brawler, a fighter, a policeman, an ice thug, a goon) for the Boston Bruins. What did he do when he was not playing hockey?*
A. *He constructed dollhouses.*

THE RINK

Are all rinks the same size?
Almost all NHL and college rinks measure 200 feet long and 85 feet wide. However, "olympic" rinks and the rinks used in Hockey USA leagues are wider.

How high are the "boards" that surround the rink?
The boards are 4′ high. The height of the plexiglass varies from rink to rink but a popular height for the glass on the ends of the rink is 10′ making the total 14′.
The glass on the sides varies also but a popular height is 6′, making the total 10′.

Must all doors in the rink swing in (away from the ice)?
Yes, for the safety of the players.

How far from the boards at the end of the rink is the goal line?
Fifteen feet.

What are the dimensions of the goal?
Six feet wide by four feet high. It is 44″ deep at the bottom and 18″ deep at the top.

What is the "goalie's crease"?
This is a light-blue semicircle in front of the goal mouth. This is the goalie's "territory," which he protects, often ferociously.

What are the dimensions of the goalie's crease?
It's a semicircle with a six-foot radius.

What's the distance from the goal line to the nearest blue line?
Sixty feet. [The distance from the goal to the center (red) line is 89′ (60′ to the blue line and 29′ from the blue line to the center line).]
(See figures 1 through 4.)

THE GAME

How long is a game?
Sixty minutes, divided into three 20-minute periods on the clock.

How long is the break between periods?
Fifteen minutes in the NHL, 12 in the NCAA (National Collegiate Athletic Association).

How many players on a team?
Eighteen skaters plus two goalies. The NCAA allows three goalies.

Do teams alternate ends of the rink each period?

Yes, but the goal judges (the officials who determine whether or not a goal is a goal) remain stationary.

How many timeouts is each team allowed during the entire game?

The NHL allows each team one 30-second timeout. In the NCAA each team gets one 60-second timeout.

What happens when a game ends in a tie?

In the NHL, after a two-minute rest (three-minute rest in the NCAA), the teams play one five-minute sudden death period. If the score is still tied after this, the game ends in a tie.

What's "sudden death"?

In an overtime period, the first team to score a goal wins the game. It's "sudden death" for the losing team.

Are tie games allowed in a playoff?

No. Players receive a 15-minute break, new ice is made and they play a 20-minute sudden death period (10 minutes in the NCAA). If the score is still tied, the process is repeated until one team scores.

How many alternate captains can a team have?

Two.

Why does a team always want to have their captain, or one of his alternates, on the ice at all times?

Because these players are the only ones allowed to speak to the ref.

Under what condition can a coach, manager, or trainer enter the rink?

When a player is injured. But they must first secure the permission of the ref.

Icing

What is "icing"?

In the NHL, icing occurs when all of the following conditions are met:

1. a defending player touches the puck
2. after the puck has crossed his own extended goal line,
3. after an opposing player has shot the puck from his own half of the rink,
4. and the puck has not touched a player on either side before it crossed the extended goal line;
5. and no defensive player (not the goalie) *could* have played the puck before it crossed the extended goal line;
6. and the team which shot the puck was not playing shorthanded.

In the NCAA, icing is the same except that no defending player has to touch the puck after it has crossed the extended goal line. The assistant ref and linesman will call icing the instant the puck crosses the line. (See figure 10.)

When is icing not called?

1. When the team shooting the puck is shorthanded.
2. When a defending player *could* have intercepted the puck before it went over his goal line.
3. If, on the way down the ice, the puck touches a defending player, his stick, or his skates before it crosses the goal line.
4. If the puck touches the goalie, his stick, or skates before it crosses the goal line.
5. If a member of the team that shot the puck reaches the puck *before* one of his opponents touches the puck. This applies only in the NHL, not in the NCAA.

6. If the puck passes through the goal crease.
7. If the puck enters the net and a score results.
8. If the puck crosses the goal line directly from a face-off.

In a shorthanded situation, the player in the penalty box deliberately stays in the box a few seconds after his penalty is served. He sees that his team, shorthanded, has shot the puck the length of the ice into the opponents' end. He figures if his team is shorthanded, the ref will not call "icing." Is he correct?

No, icing *will* be called. The team's shorthanded status ends by the clock, not when the player decides to leave the penalty box.

OFFSIDE

What is offside?

1. Offside is when a player who does not have possession and control of the puck crosses the opponents' blue line ahead of the puck. The puck must already be across the blue line and inside the opponents' defending zone before he, himself, can cross the blue line. However, if the player has possession of the puck, he is *not* offside when he crosses the opponents' blue line and enters their defending zone.
2. A player is offside if *both* his skates (not his body or his stick) are over the opponents' blue line before the puck is.
3. But he's not offside if only one of his skates is over the blue line. That's why a player can straddle the blue line and not be offside.
4. No player on the attacking team can cross the opponents' blue line ahead of the puck.
5. If the defending team can shoot the puck *back across* its own blue line and into the neutral zone, all the

attacking players must vacate the attacking zone before their team can again bring the puck back over the opponents' blue line. (See figures 8 and 9.)

6. In the NHL, a player is offside if he receives the puck after it has traveled across two lines: his own blue line and the red line, or the red line and the opponents' blue line. This constitutes an *offside pass,* sometimes called a *"two-line pass."* The official will blow his whistle, stop play and order a face-off. There is no penalty. (See figure 11.)

7. In the NCAA, you *can* pass over two lines: your own blue line and the red line that bisects the rink.

Why should a player be penalized for being offside?

You'd agree, wouldn't you, that hockey would be a pretty dull game if a team were allowed to station one or more of its players right in front of the opposing goal. To prevent this from happening, and to force a team to *work* the puck into their attacking zone by astute passing, forechecking, or effective stickwork, several rules have been developed. When a referee sees a player offside, he blows his whistle, declares "offside" and stops the game temporarily.

If a player's stick is over the blue line, is he offside?

No, both his skates must be over the line for him to be offside.

What is another term for the official's call of "delayed offside"?

"Slow whistle." (See figure 12.)

FACE-OFFS

Where can a face-off occur?

Any place on the rink except within 15 feet of the goal or the boards.

During a face-off, are any players other than the two players facing off allowed inside the circle or within 15 feet of the face-off?
No.

What happens if the player who is supposed to face-off does not get into position promptly?
The official can replace him with another player.

Before the face-off, must the blades of the sticks of the two face-off opponents be on the ice?
Yes.

What if a player, behind his own net with the puck, wants to start up the ice but he's bottled up by his opponents who block his forward progress. If he does nothing, simply remaining behind the net with the puck, waiting for the opponents to leave him alone so he can proceed unmolested, how long can he remain motionless behind his own net, trying to wait out his opponents?
Hockey prides itself on being a fast game and abhors unnecessary delays. If the player delays at all, the ref will order a face-off. Thus the player loses control of the puck for delaying the game. If it happens again, there is the possibility of a two-minute minor delay of game penalty.

Your player is penalized in my *defending zone. Where will the face-off be?*
In the neutral zone.

If your player is penalized in your *defending zone, where will the face-off be?*
Near where the penalty occurred, on a face-off dot or in line with the dot, but at least 15 feet from the boards and the nearest goal.

RULES FOR GOALIES

Can the goalie participate in play beyond the center red line?
No.

Can a goalie pass the puck to a teammate with his hands? With his stick?
Hands, no. Stick, yes.

Is the goalie allowed to throw the puck?
Yes, but not forward.

MORE QUESTIONS ABOUT THE RULES OF THE GAME

If one of your players breaks his stick, may one of the players on your bench toss him a replacement?
No. He must skate over to the bench and be handed a replacement stick.

If a player on the other side loses possession of his stick and it drops to the ice, can one of your players kick it or push it to keep it away from him?
No, and your player will get a two-minute penalty if he does.

Running around the entire interior circumference of the rink are vertical slats, called "boards," which extend from below the ice surface to 40" above the ice. On top of the "boards" is a horizontal surface, a "ledge" about five inches wide. What if the puck comes to rest on this horizontal surface of the boards. Is the puck still in play?
Yes. Any player can knock it back onto the ice with his stick or his hand.

What happens when the puck gets stuck in the netting in the back of the goal?

Play is stopped and the puck is faced off. If the defending team shot the puck on the net, the face-off will be on either of the face-off dots in that team's defending zone. If the offensive team shot the puck on the back of the net, the face-off will be outside the blue line in the neutral zone.

Is a puck on the back of the net considered playable?

Yes. But if it remains on the net for more than three seconds, play will be stopped.

Regarding "handling the puck," which of the following are not permitted?
  1. *A player may stop it with his skate.*
  2. *He can kick it with his skate.*
  3. *He can stop it with any part of his body.*
  4. *He can carry it.*
  5. *He can hold it with his hand.*
  6. *He can catch it and drop it immediately.*
  7. *He can bat it with his hand if he is the first player to recover the puck.*
  8. *He can hit the puck in the air with his stick or hand.*
  9. *He can stop it on the ice with his hand.*
 10. *He can "hand pass" it in his defending zone.*

All are legal except 4 and 5, which will earn a two-minute penalty.

Batting the puck by holding your stick more than four feet above the ice is illegal, except in what circumstances?
  1. If you bat the puck to an opponent.
  2. If you bat the puck into your own goal. (The goal counts.)
  3. If the *goalie* "high sticks" the puck.

Larry Murphy and coach Bob Johnson (© Michael DiGirolamo/BBS)

Is kicking a puck permitted?
Yes, but a kicked goal does not count.

What is a "kick shot"?
This is using your leg and foot to propel the stick's blade, often resulting in a dangerous shot (considered dangerous because a kicked stick can break and splinter, especially when kicked by a razor sharp skate). In the NCAA this will be rewarded with a misconduct penalty.

Can a player have physical contact with an opposing player on any and every part of the rink or is he limited to making contact to certain sections of the rink?
Under NHL rules players can "check" (make legal physical contact) with opponents anywhere on the rink.

Who is allowed to sit on the bench?
Players in uniform, the manager, coach, and trainer.

In baseball, if a player wants to retie his shoe laces, he just requests the umpire to call "time out." How does hockey differ?
Regardless of what happens to a hockey player's equipment, the ref will not stop the game. It's up to the player to maintain his equipment. In the NCAA, a player who loses his helmet must put it back on and skate directly to his team's bench.

Is play stopped when the goal comes loose from its post?
Yes.

How is the goal secured to the ice?
Before 1991, the metal goal frame was held in position on the ice by magnets. These magnets proved so ineffective that goal posts came loose an average of six times each game. Since 1991, the metal goal frame has been held in place by a flexible rubber peg which is attached securely to the ice and projects 8″ up inside the hollow goal post The

rubber pegs hold the goal frame in position yet provide some "give" when players hit the net with their bodies. Goals now come loose only about once a game.

The latest method of securing the goal to the ice is through "breakaway" posts.

Must there be a minimum number of players on the ice at any one time from each team?

Yes, each team must have at least three skaters (not including the goalie) regardless how many penalties it has. All penalized players must leave the ice and go to the penalty box. To maintain three skaters, the coach may have to add players from the bench.

The red line bisects the rink. When was it introduced to the game?

The red line was introduced during World War II to speed up play, increase scoring, and thereby boost declining attendance. Previously, a defending team was often locked into its own defending zone because it had to *stickhandle* (not pass) the puck over its own blue line. Adding the "red line" enabled the team to *pass* the puck over their own blue line, up to the red line.

In the NCAA, is a college band allowed to play while the game is in progress?

No. If they continue to play, their team may receive a two-minute bench penalty.

If a player leaves the penalty box before his time is served, what happens?

The ref will wait until the player's team gains possession of the puck and then stop play. He will order a face-off in the defending zone of that team.

Does the home team have its choice of ends at the start of the game?

Yes.

What is the maximum time allotted for the pregame warmup?

Twenty minutes in the NHL, but only 15 in the NCAA.

Why would a player want to give his stick to another player who has broken his stick?

If the *goalie* broke his stick and action was concentrated around his goal, it would be good strategy for a forward to give his stick to the goalie so the goalie could at least have *some* type of stick. Then the forward could race to his bench to get a replacement stick. When play stops, the goalie can get a proper replacement goalie stick.

What's the rule regarding the wearing of a helmet?

All players must wear a helmet, but a player can apply to the League Office for exemption. In the NCAA, helmets with secure chin straps are mandatory.

What is the rule regarding fighting?

The NHL rule book says, "A major penalty (five minutes) shall be imposed on any player who engages in fisticuffs." In addition, the ref could assess the fighting player(s) an additional major, minor, and/or game misconduct penalty. The rule book goes on to say that the instigator of a fight will be assessed a game misconduct.

In the NCAA, a player who starts a fight is given a disqualification penalty, which banishes him for the remainder of the game.

DIFFERENT LEAGUES, DIFFERENT RULES

Which leagues play by the "pro" rules?

NHL and amateur leagues in the US and Canada. Some other leagues play by the "pro" rules with minor differences.

Which leagues do not use the pro rules?

Colleges, US high schools, Olympic Games, and the International Ice Hockey Federation each play under different rules. The NCAA has its own rule book which is followed by all colleges. Most rules of adult hockey leagues are quite similar.

What are the major differences between the NCAA and the NHL rule books regarding icing, offside, bodychecking, and fighting?

1. *Icing.* In the NCAA, icing occurs the instant the puck crosses the goal line. But in the NHL, icing does not occur until the puck has crossed the goal line and is touched by a player on the defending team, other than the goalie.

2. *Offside.* Under NCAA rules, a player can pass all the way to his opponent's blue line. In the NHL, there is a red line which cuts the rink in half. In the NHL, a pass over any two lines is offside: your own blue line and the red line, or over the red line and your opponent's blue line. Either of these passes would be offside in the NHL.

3. *Fighting.* Under college rules, a player is expelled from that game plus his team's next game for fighting. In the NHL, "fisticuffs" warrants only a major penalty. The penalties for spearing and butt-ending are similar in both the NHL and NCAA. (See the next chapter for descriptions of the penalties.)

RULES THAT APPLY ONLY IN COLLEGE GAMES (NCAA)

In the NCAA, what happens if either the players or the fans become unruly?

The ref may stop the game at any time and, unless two periods have been completed, it is "no game."

How many officials in the NCAA can call a penalty?
    Three, as of 1996. The "head ref," the one who wears an armband, is primarily responsible for calling a penalty. Both the assistant ref and the linesman are responsible for calling offside and icing. However, these two *can* call a penalty that the head ref does not see. (In the NHL, a linesman cannot stop play to call a penalty unless it is a major penalty "of a serious incident" which he has observed and which he is sure that the referee did not see.)

Chapter 4
PENALTIES

Think of it: Hockey is the only sport that arms its players with both protective padding and a stick, confines play inside a four-foot-high wall, and provides its players with the ability to accelerate to 25 MPH. Maybe those are some of the reasons why this game has so many different types of penalties (and why this is the longest chapter of the book)!

Q. *Why did New York Ranger Rod Gilbert say, "When I was a kid, you didn't want to be a goalie in the spring"?*
A. *In the old days, street hockey pucks hadn't been invented yet, so kids used "road apples" (frozen horse droppings) which they molded into the shape of a puck.*

THE THEORY BEHIND PENALIZING A PLAYER OR A TEAM

In football you can penalize by giving or denying a team yardage, in basketball by awarding free throws, and in baseball by calling the offending player "out." Since none of these would work in hockey, the officials penalize a team mainly by requiring the offending team to play temporarily with fewer players than their opponent.

PENALTIES IN THE NHL

What are the classifications *of penalties in the NHL?*
1. *Minor.* Two minutes. No player may be substituted for the offending player.
2. *Bench minor.* Two minutes. Any player may serve the penalty, even someone on the bench when the infraction occurred.
3. *Major.* Five minutes. No substitution. Usually received for fighting, or when a player draws blood from his opponent while committing an illegal action. If a player receives three major penalties in the same game, he is expelled from the game and a substitute player may play for him after five minutes.
4. *Misconduct.* Ten minutes. Substitution is allowed immediately. Usually received for abusive language or gesture.
5. *Game misconduct.* Suspension for the remainder of the game, but a sub may play for the suspended player immediately.
6. *Gross misconduct.* Can be assessed upon a player, manager, coach, or trainer. Suspension for the remainder of the game. Case will be referred to the league president.
7. *Match.* Suspension for the remainder of the game. When levied upon a player for *deliberately attempting* to injure an opponent, a sub can play for him after five minutes.
8. *Penalty shot.* See details on page 54.

TYPES OF PENALTIES IN THE NHL

Which ten infractions can be either a two-minute minor penalty or a five-minute major penalty, depending upon their severity?

1. Fighting
2. Hooking
3. High sticking
4. Elbowing
5. Kneeing

6. Spearing
7. Cross-checking
8. Charging
9. Boarding
10. Slashing

(Read on for descriptions of each.)

DESCRIPTION OF SPECIFIC PENALTIES

What happens when a player legally checks an opponent by using his own stick to hook his opponent's stick?
There's no penalty. Stick-to-stick contact is considered neither hooking nor holding.

What happens when you "run interference" for the puck carrier on your team (skating directly in front of him and attempting to "take out" any opposing player who tries either to stop the puck carrier or take the puck away from him)?
You will be penalized for interference. But the good news is that this penalty is infrequently called.

What happens when you stop the progress of a player who is not in possession of the puck?
That's interference. However, if you are playing defensively, you have a right to stand your ground.

What is "handling the puck with your hands"?
When a player closes his hand around the puck (unless he's the goalie). If he does, it's a two-minute penalty.

What's the penalty if a player deliberately falls on the puck to cover it with his body?
Two-minute penalty. But if a defending player does it within the goal crease, a penalty shot will be awarded.

What penalty does a player face when he "mouths off" at an official?

A misconduct penalty. But if he is assessed a minor penalty and then mouths off, he is assessed both the minor penalty *and* the misconduct penalty.

What is a board check? Does it call for a penalty?

When a player deliberately checks another player into the boards, that is a board check and calls for a penalty. By the rules, it calls for a minor penalty but the ref must use much discretion. If one player just rides another into the boards, that's not a penalty. It's a difficult call for a ref.

Is it a penalty to play with a broken stick?

Yes. A two-minute minor. A player cannot continue to hold on to his broken stick. He must drop it on the ice. However, the *goalie* can continue to play with a broken stick until the next stoppage of play when an official will remove the broken stick from the ice.

What is charging?

Charging is when a player takes more than two strides in the direction of the opponent he checks. It can be a minor or a major penalty.

What is cross-checking?

When a player holds his stick parallel to the ice with his hands about two feet apart on the shaft and then thrusts this very solid part of his stick against an opponent's arm, chest, or back.

What is butt-ending?

When a player thrusts the shaft end of his stick (the end opposite to the blade) into the body of an opponent.

What happens when a player uses his knees or elbows to fend off an opponent?

He is given a two-minute penalty.

What is "high sticking"?

High sticking occurs when a player carries his stick above the height of his opponent's waist and touches his opponent with it. If injury results, the guilty player is assessed a double minor penalty when the injury is judged to be accidental. When the injury is judged to be a result of carelessness, the guilty player can be assessed a major and a game misconduct penalty. High sticking usually happens when a player is trying to intercept a puck that's high in the air. Or when he's trying to hit an opponent.

If a player high sticks another player and draws blood, what happens?

The offending player receives a five-minute major penalty and possible suspension for the remainder of the game. He must stay off the ice for the full five minutes regardless of the number of goals the opponents score. In the NHL, the offending player must leave the ice for the remainder of the game, if the injury was judged to be "careless." In the NCAA, if the injury is judged to be intentional, the offending player is suspended for the remainder of the game plus his team's next game.

What if the player intentionally high sticks to an opponent's face or head, but draws no blood?

The same penalty is assessed.

If an attacking player high sticks a puck and it goes into the net, does the goal count?

Not if he high sticked above the height of the goal.

What if a defensive player high sticks the puck above the height of the goal and the puck goes into the net. Does the goal count?

Yes.

If you high stick the puck and it goes to a player on your own team, what happens?

The ref blows his whistle, stops play, and calls for a face-off.

What if you high stick the puck and it goes to an opponent?
What then?

Play continues.

*If a player, pursuing an opponent who has control of the
puck, catches him by hooking his stick around the opponent's stomach, what's the call?*

That's hooking, a two-minute minor penalty.

*If the opponent did not have control of the puck, what's the
call?*

That's interference, a two-minute minor penalty.

What is interference?

Interference is impeding an opponent who does not have
the puck. This is the technical explanation, but the truth is
that most interference situations do not result in a penalty
and many interference situations are called by other
names: high sticking, holding, etc.

What is slashing?

When a player uses his stick to make a slashing motion
aimed at an opponent. Even if there's no contact, the
motion itself is sufficient for a two-minute penalty.

What is spearing?

Stabbing an opponent with the blade end of your stick.
This is an automatic major penalty.

When is tripping called?

It's called when you cause your opponent to trip by using
your stick, foot, arm, elbow, knee, or hand.

When is tripping not called?

In two main situations. One is when your opponent trips
by stepping on his *own* stick. The second is when he trips
as you are trying to gain possession of the puck by hook-
checking.

What's a "bench penalty"?

This is a two-minute penalty usually assessed for abusive language or other breach of conduct from players on the bench, or for too many players on the ice. Anyone on the bench may serve the penalty.

What is the penalty for delaying the game?

Two minutes.

Can one player grab the jersey of another? Can he put his arm around the neck of another? Can he hold another player with his stick?

No. Each of these illegal actions is considered holding, a two-minute penalty.

Does the NHL permit fights?

The NHL rule book says, "The Referee is provided very wide latitude in the penalties which he may impose under this rule. . . ." Penalties can range from a minor penalty to a major and game misconduct penalty. The instigator and the "brawler" receive the harshest penalties.

Severe Penalties
(penalties of at least five minutes)

What are the names of the severe penalties?

1. Major
2. Misconduct
3. Game misconduct
4. Gross misconduct
5. Match
6. Penalty shot.

What is the most severe penalty?

A player who receives either a game misconduct penalty or a match penalty is suspended for the remainder of the game.

Can a player ever face disciplinary action from the league?

Yes. In the NCAA a player is not fined but he can be suspended not only for the remainder of the current game but the next game also and under certain conditions for future games.

In the NHL, the suspended player can be fined by the league in addition to being suspended for the remainder of the current game and future games.

How long is a misconduct penalty? Can a player be substituted?

Ten minutes. Yes, a player can be substituted immediately.

What infraction is so serious that an automatic goal is awarded to the other team?

Suppose you have a breakaway on an open net, a sure goal for you. But suddenly someone from the other team throws a stick onto the ice, hits the puck, and you are prevented from shooting at the open net. Justice prevails; the ref awards you the goal.

Why is there so much fighting in hockey?

Hockey is the only game played with such intensity, where players move so fast, where each is armed with a stick, where the playing surface is so small relative to the speed which players move and where the game is confined to such a small space, relatively.

Fighting has always been a characteristic of the game.

In the NHL, if the player who starts the fight happens to be wearing a face shield, does it make any difference?

Yes, he is assessed an additional minor penalty.

If a team's players are engaged in a fight between periods, or before or after a game, how much is the team fined by the NHL?

Twenty-five thousand dollars-plus.

During a bench-clearing brawl, what happens to the first player to leave the bench to join the fight?

In the NCAA, every player who leaves the bench when a fight is in progress will be assessed a disqualification penalty, suspended from that game and the following game, and will receive a major penalty.

In the NHL, the first and second players to leave the bench receive a game misconduct penalty. The first player to leave the bench from either or both teams will be suspended automatically without pay for the next ten games his team plays. The second (and any other players) to leave the bench in order to fight will be suspended automatically without pay for the next five games. In addition, the league assesses fines to the teams of those who fought.

What happens to a player who charges an official and makes contact with him?

In the NHL, he receives a game misconduct penalty. If the official is injured, the player will be suspended for three to 20 games depending upon the intent and severity of the injury. In the NCAA, he gets a five-minute major plus a "disqualification" penalty (meaning he sits out the rest of the game).

What if the player says nothing verbally but gestures obscenely?

Same penalty, game misconduct.

If a player receives a ten-minute misconduct penalty, does his team play shorthanded?

No. A substitute is allowed, but the penalized player must stay in the penalty box for ten minutes, regardless of any goals scored by the opposition.

If two players are fighting and a third player joins in, what penalties are assessed?

The two fighting originally each get five-minute major penalties. The "third man in" gets a game misconduct penalty. He cannot return to the ice for the entire game.

The "third man in" heavy penalty is designed to prevent bench-clearing brawls.

What if a player in the penalty box leaves the box to join a fight in progress?

He continues with his original penalty and is additionally assessed a double minor plus a game misconduct penalty. The purpose of these severe added penalties, again, is to restrict the fight to those already on the ice and to avoid a bench-clearing brawl.

Q. *What were the most penalty minutes ever meted out in a single NHL game?*

A. *The 406 minutes in a 1981 game between Boston and Minnesota. After the penalties were assessed and the severest offenders were suspended, the Bruins had eight players available and the North Stars had nine.*

What happens to a player who deliberately injures an official, manager, or trainer?

He's suspended from that game and probably future games, at the discretion of the league.

When a player receives a major and a minor penalty at the same time, which does he serve first?

In almost all cases, he will serve the major first.

What penalty is assessed "for attempting to injure"?

A five-minute penalty. No substitute is allowed.

What's the penalty if a defending player, not the goalie, falls on the puck or picks up the puck while it's in the goal crease?

The most severe penalty of all—a penalty shot! (Read on for the details. See page 54.)

When two players fight, does the player who started the fight get a longer penalty?

They usually get the same penalty regardless of who started the fight.

If any offensive player is held inside the goalie's crease by a defending player, is this a penalty?

No.

When a player fights with a spectator, what penalty does he receive?

Game misconduct.

If a player touches or holds any official, is it a penalty?

You bet! Either a ten-minute misconduct or a game misconduct. Plus he'll sit out a few games.

Match Penalty

(There is no "match penalty" in the NCAA. However, unique to college rules is the "disqualification penalty," which will be explained toward the end of the chapter.)

In the NHL a match penalty involves the suspension of the player for the rest of the game. Can a substitute play for him? Must the team play shorthanded?

A substitute must wait five minutes before he can play if the penalized player deliberately attempted to injure but failed to do so. If he deliberately injured another, the guilty player, in addition to receiving a match penalty, will be suspended from further competition until the League Commissioner has ruled on the deed.

If the opponents score before the above penalties are served, are the penalties forgiven? Are the players allowed to return to the ice?

No.

Does a team play shorthanded when one of its members receives a match penalty?

Yes.

Suppose that at the end of a fight, and as they are breaking up, one player kicks his skate at the other. Is this a penalty?

This calls for a match penalty even if the kicking player made no contact. In addition, he faces possible suspension for future games. Kicking is regarded as a serious infraction.

In a fight, when a player head butts his opponent, what's the penalty?

Match penalty, five minutes, no substitute allowed. If his opponent is severely injured, it's a ten-minute penalty.

If a player has three major penalties in one game, what happens to him?

He is suspended and cannot return to the game. However, a substitute can replace him after five minutes.

Game Misconduct Penalty

What is a game misconduct penalty?

The player is suspended for the balance of the game but a substitute is allowed to play immediately.

MORE QUESTIONS ABOUT PENALTIES IN THE NHL

What's the rule regarding "fake flops" or "diving," a ploy intended to draw a penalty on an opponent?

It's now a two-minute penalty for taking a fake flop via a "phantom trip" or hook. This holds true in the NCAA also.

The Stanley Cup (© Bruce Bennett Studios)

Q. *How many cans of soda would the top piece of the Stanley Cup hold?*
A. *About eight 12-ounce cans.*

What's the "sin bin"?
"Sin bin" is just another name for the penalty box.

Do all minor penalties result in "two minutes in the penalty box"?
Yes. However, in a power play, if the team with the player advantage scores, the penalized player will be released from his penalty and can return to the ice without serving the remainder of his penalty.

After the penalized player serves his two minute penalty, may he return to the ice immediately?
Yes.

What are "coincidental minor penalties"?
When a player from each team is penalized, usually for the same "minor" infraction, and their penalties start and end at the same time on the game clock.

Do both teams play shorthanded?
In this situation, no substitution is allowed for the penalized players. Since "shorthanded" means that one team plays with fewer players than the other, neither team will be shorthanded. If the penalties were given when both teams were at full strength, each team would then play with only four skaters.

Your team is leading late in the game and you're seeking to delay the game. You have the puck. You're alone and you freeze it against the boards. Any problem?
You'd receive a two-minute penalty for "delaying the game."

One of your players intentionally drops his gloves and stick on the ice. Is this OK?
Nope. Looks like he wants to fight. A two-minute penalty.

To defend your goal against a shot from an opponent, you drop to your knees in an attempt to block the shot. The puck gets caught in your equipment, and you can't dislodge it. Will you be penalized?
No.

While attempting to bat down a puck with your stick, you raise your stick above the level of your shoulders. Any problem?
It's OK to bat a puck down with a high stick. No penalty. Play will continue if an opposing player is the first to touch the batted down puck. But if the first one to touch the puck is you or any member of your team, the ref will blow his whistle, stop play, and call a face-off.

Can a player hit the puck with his hand while it's in the air?
Yes, if he merely knocks it straight down.

What happens if a penalty occurs with less than two minutes remaining in a period?
The remainder of the penalty carries over to the beginning of the second, third, or overtime period.

What would be considered "dumb" penalties?
The first type of "dumb" penalty would be when you allow your man to get by you in your defending zone and you are forced to resort to illegal methods to slow him down. Usually this is done by hooking or tripping him.

The second type of "dumb" penalty would be when you are in your attacking zone and you get caught doing something illegal, usually needlessly. After all, your opponent can't score if you've got him bottled up in his defending zone!

The third situation is when your team has a man advantage due to an opposing player having been confined to the penalty box, and then you or someone on your team commits a penalty and you immediately lose your man advantage.

How many penalties are called in an average game?
About 11.

What are the total penalty minutes in an average game?
Twenty-five minutes. Season averages for NHL teams range from 18 minutes to 30 minutes per game.

If an injured player who is in need of first aid also receives a penalty, who serves it for him?
The coach selects a player to sit in the penalty box while the injured player receives medical attention.

What does "killing a penalty " mean?
Your team "kills a penalty" when it prevents the opposing team from scoring during those minutes when your team is forced to play shorthanded because of a penalty. When your team is shorthanded, the opposing team has a "power play."

What is an effective "penalty killing" average for a NHL team?
An excellent penalty killing team will "kill off" 83 percent of their opponents' power plays. This means they will not allow their opponents to score while they have a power play. But even a team with a league-low average of 74 percent still manages to "kill off" three of every four power plays of their opponents.

Can a player legally push the puck along the ice with his hand? Can he pass it to a teammate?
Yes, but only in his defending zone.

GOALIE PENALTIES

In hockey, does the player who receives the penalty have to sit out the penalty in the sin bin or can some other player serve it in his place?

No substitute is allowed to serve a two-minute minor or a five-minute major penalty. But goalies are an exception, and so are injured players.

Does a goalie ever serve a minor, major, or misconduct penalty?
No. In the NHL, it is served by some other player.

When is a goalie ruled off the ice in the NHL?
If he commits three major penalties in one game, or just one game misconduct or one match penalty.

Can a goalie ever be disqualified from a game?
Yes. In the NCAA, if a goalie receives a disqualification penalty, he is banned from the remainder of the game, and a substitute goalie will play in his place. In the NHL, if the goalie is penalized for intending to injure another player (like whacking him with his stick) he can be banned from the rest of the game.

Is a goalie penalized for leaving his crease if there's a fight on the ice?
Yes. He will receive a two-minute minor if he strays near the fight area.

Can the goalie throw the puck toward the opposing goal?
No, he can only throw it to the side.

If the goalie, under intense pressure from the other team, deliberately lifts the puck into the seats to slow down the pace of the game, is there a penalty?
Yes, two minutes for delay of game.

If the goalie, facing a breakaway by a player from the opposing team, deliberately displaces the goal post, what's the penalty?
A penalty shot.

If there is no breakaway, and the goalie displaces the goal post deliberately, what's the penalty?
A two-minute minor penalty.

THE PENALTY SHOT

What is a penalty shot?

It is a scoring opportunity for the attacking team whereby there is a one-on-one situation, involving one attacking player and the defending goalie. All other players are excluded from the ice. (See figure 14.)

When is a team awarded a penalty shot?

When any of the following happen:

1. A defending player, not the goalie, falls on the puck when it is in the crease.
2. A player throws a stick at an opposing player who has a clear chance to score.
3. A player fouls another player from behind when that player has a clear shot at the goal. In the NCAA, the player must have been in the attacking zone (over the blue line) when the penalty occurs.
4. A player deliberately displaces the goal post when an opposing player has a breakaway.
5. A player deliberately displaces the goal post within the last two minutes of play.
6. A defending player, other than the goalie, picks up the puck inside the crease.
7. A player illegally enters the game in the last two minutes of play.
8. A player throws his stick at the puck, in his defending zone.

What does it mean to "illegally enter" a game?

Illegally entering a game could be:

1. When there are too many players on the ice after the player enters.
2. The player's name was not on the score sheet at the beginning of the game.

FIGURE 14.   The Penalty Shot: One of the most exciting events in hockey, but it happens very infrequently. For additional information, see page 54.

3. A penalized player left the penalty box before his penalty was over.

Who may take the penalty shot?

In most situations, any player designated by his coach who was on the ice at the time of the penalty. However, if a player was hauled down from behind, that player is awarded the penalty shot.

How many shots can the player take on the goalie?

He gets one shot. No rebounds may be attempted.

On a penalty shot, when may the goalie leave his crease?
As soon as the opposing player, who starts at center ice, touches the puck.

When a player takes a penalty shot, when is his scoring opportunity ended?
When the puck crosses the goal line or when the player has taken his shot. He gets only one shot and can play no rebounds.

How often is a penalty shot granted by a referee?
In an entire NHL season, referees on average award only about 15 penalty shots.

How many penalty shots are converted into scored goals?
Of 15 penalty shots awarded, six or seven will result in goals.

SHORTHANDED

When is a team "shorthanded?"
A team is shorthanded when it has fewer skaters than its opponent. A team could be shorthanded by one skater (5–4 or 4–3) or shorthanded by two skaters (5–3).

A player for your team and my team each receive a two-minute minor penalty, both at the same time. Now both teams have only four skaters. Is either team "shorthanded"?
No. A team is shorthanded when it has fewer skaters than its opponent. In this situation, both teams have an equal number of skaters, so neither team is shorthanded. Neither team can receive any of the benefits of being short-handed, such as not being called for icing.

Is a team entitled to have a minimum number of players on ice, even though it has been heavily penalized?

A team is entitled to have three skaters regardless of the number of penalties it has been assessed.

What if your team already has two players in the penalty box and you're playing two men shorthanded—and then a third player is penalized. Do you play three men short?
No. Regardless of how many penalties a team might have against it, it is entitled to always have three skaters on the ice.

Under what condition is a player released from the penalty box before his penalty time is up?
If his team is playing shorthanded and the opponents score, he is free to leave the penalty box. The remainder of his penalty is forgiven.

A player on my team receives two two-minute minor penalties. Fifty seconds later, your team scores. Is my player free to return to the ice?
No. He is "forgiven" for the 70 seconds remaining on his first two-minute penalty. But he must immediately begin to serve his second two-minute penalty.

Does the player who receives the penalty have to sit out the penalty or can someone else serve it for him?
No substitute is allowed to serve a two-minute minor penalty or a five-minute major. Goalies are an exception.

A player is in the penalty box serving a ten-minute misconduct penalty. When his ten-minutes are up, can he immediately jump back onto the ice and begin playing?
No. He must wait until play stops. It's possible that his penalty could last another one or two minutes until play stops. But remember, the penalized player has been substituted for during his ten-minute penalty. His team has not been playing shorthanded because of his penalty.

Q. *What's the longest single game shutout?*
A. *Goalie Norm Smith of the Detroit Red Wings turned away 92 shots in a 1–0 playoff game between Detroit and the Montreal Maroons on March 25, 1936. It was the longest game in history, extending five hours, 51 minutes. The game's only goal came at the seventeenth minute of the sixth overtime period.*

If a team is serving a two-minute minor penalty, playing one man shorthanded, and the opposing team scores a goal, what happens?

The shorthanded team immediately goes back to full strength. The penalty is erased.

This time a team is serving a major five-minute penalty. They are a man short, and the opposing team scores a goal. Is the penalized player free to leave the penalty box? Is the team now at full strength? Is the five-minute penalty forgiven?

No, the penalty is not forgiven. The team will still play with a man short. The opposing team can score as many goals as they are able. The penalized team will play the entire five minutes a man short.

A team commits a minor penalty and player A goes to the penalty box for two minutes. A few seconds later the team commits an additional two-minute penalty. Now they have two players in the box, player A and player B, and are playing shorthanded two players. The opposing team scores a goal. Can both of the penalized players return to the ice?

No. Only player A can return. However, if the opposing team scores a second goal, player B may return before his two minutes are up. The first player *in* the box is the first player *out* of the box.

When a player receives a major penalty, he's required to sit in the penalty box for five minutes. Can a player be substituted for him?

No. His team must play shorthanded for five minutes.

If the opponents score during the five-minute major penalty, is the penalized player excused? Can he return to the ice?

No, he must stay in the box for the full penalty, regardless of the number of times the opponents score.

A player on your team and my team get into a fight. Both are assessed five-minute major penalties. Do both of our teams play a man short for the five minutes?

No. In this situation, both of our teams play full strength. The penalties cancel each other. In the NCAA, both players are ejected.

Who makes sure that penalized players actually serve their time in the penalty box?

One of the officials at every game is the "penalty time keeper." As boss of the penalty box, it's his job to make sure that every penalized player serves his time.

PENALTIES IN THE *NCAA*

Although the rule books of the NHL and NCAA are very similar, when it comes to the subject of penalties there are significant differences. In the following pages, an attempt will be made to explain what is unique about penalty rules in the NCAA.

What are the classification of penalties in the NCAA?

1. Minor
2. Bench minor
3. Major
4. Misconduct
5. Disqualification
6. Penalty shot
7. Game misconduct

How do NCAA rules differ from NHL rules?

A major difference is that the NCAA rules have a "disqualification" penalty and no "gross misconduct" or "match" penalty.

What's the difference between a major and a minor penalty in the number of minutes a player must serve in the penalty box?

Minor penalties are for two minutes, major penalties are for five minutes.

What are the usual "minor" two-minute penalties in the NCAA?

1. Tripping
2. Holding
3. Playing with a broken stick
4. Delaying the game
5. Roughing
6. Handling the puck with your hands
7. Interference
8. High sticking
9. Slashing
10. Charging
11. Cross-checking
12. Elbowing
13. Boarding

NCAA Severe Penalties

In the NCAA, what are the nine ways a player can receive a "misconduct" penalty?

1. Using foul or abusive language during or following a game.
2. Interfering with a penalty shot.
3. Disputing a decision, not going to the penalty box directly, showing disrespect for the ref.
4. Using a "kick shot." This is a method of propelling the puck by placing it next to your stick blade and then kicking the stick.
5. Trying to prevent a breakaway attempt on your team's goal by jumping on the ice from either the penalty box or the players' bench.

6. Throwing a puck or stick into the spectators' area.
7. Entering or remaining in the ref's crease (see term defined in the back of the book).
8. Using an illegal stick. This also gets you a two-minute minor.
9. Shooting the puck away from an official who's trying to retrieve it.

What is the "disqualification" penalty in the NCAA?
The player not only receives a major penalty but he is suspended for both the remainder of the game and the following game. This penalty is usually charged to a player who fights or attempts to injure an opponent. The player is prohibited from sitting in the penalty box or on the players' bench while in uniform.

Who might receive a disqualification penalty?
A player who fights or attempts to injure an opponent before, during, or after the game.

Who besides a player can receive a "game misconduct" penalty?
The coach, manager, trainer, and other team personnel.

Can any of the above return to the game?
No.

In a "misconduct" penalty, can the coach substitute another player for the guilty player? Must the guilty player remain in the penalty box for the entire ten minutes?
In both cases, the answer is "yes" unless the penalized player is seriously injured and must leave the game.

Does the disqualified player serve the penalty?
No. A substitute serves the penalty. The penalized player must leave the game. While in uniform, he cannot sit on the bench or even stand in the runway.

What if a player leaves the bench to join a fight?

It's a five-minute major plus disqualification. This prohibits him from playing the remainder of that game plus his team's next game.

In a major penalty, can the guilty player be substituted for or must he serve the entire five minutes?

The guilty player must serve the entire five minutes in the penalty box unless he is ejected from the game at this point. No substitute is allowed during these five minutes. However, if the guilty player is too injured to sit in the penalty box, the coach may insert another player to sit in the penalty box in place of the guilty player.

What if the other team scores? Can he leave the penalty box and return to the ice?

No.

In "coincidental major penalties" does each team play short-handed for the five minutes? Can the coach substitute for the penalized player serving his time in the sin bin?

If coincidental major penalties are called, teams play at full strength, with only the penalized players being "punished," not their teams. The penalized players would serve five minutes in the sin bin. No substitution would be allowed. Although "coincidental major penalties" is a rare call, it would be appropriate when two players are fighting.

When a fight breaks out in a college game, what are the non-fighting players who are on the ice at the time supposed to do?

All those not fighting are to skate over to their bench. The goalie is to stay in his crease area.

In the above, what is the penalty for those who do not comply?

Each can be assessed a two-minute penalty.

If a player hits the puck with his stick above his shoulders, will he be penalized?

No penalty, but play is stopped and a face-off takes place.

What if he tries to hit the puck but misses it?

The stoppage in play is the same as if he actually hit the puck. It is a rare call.

Are these minor or major penalties: Grabbing your opponent's facemask? Headbutting him with your helmet?

You guessed right if you said "major." If the ref interprets the action to be a "deliberate attempt to injure," the offending player will receive a game misconduct penalty.

Can a team ever be penalized due to the unruliness of their home crowd?

Yes. And in the NHL, the ref may assess a two-minute penalty to the home team.

NCAA Minor Penalties

Is it a penalty to check the goalie while he's in his crease?

Yes, it is a penalty, either two minutes or five minutes.

Is it a penalty for a goalie to remove his helmet or facemask during play?

It's a two minute penalty.

You are the goalie. You're outside your crease and you fall on the puck. Is this OK?

No. You have just earned a two-minute penalty for delaying the game.

Does the goalie serve a penalty himself?

In the NCAA, the goalie does serve a *major* penalty himself. The coach can substitute a spare goalie and remove one player in addition to the starting goalie, who must sit in the penalty box during the penalty time. When the penalty is over, the player who was removed for the spare goalie can go on the ice and rejoin the game. The penalized goalie cannot go back in the goal until the spare goalie has left the ice.

DELAYED WHISTLE

What is a "delayed whistle"?

When a team has possession of the puck, and the opposing team commits a foul, the ref raises his hand but does not blow his whistle. It would be unfair to take the puck away from the team in possession of the puck at this point, so he *delays* blowing his whistle. However, the moment the opposing team gains control of the puck, he'll blow his whistle, stop play, and penalize the guilty player on the team. (See figure 15 on page 69.)

Let's say that in the "delayed whistle" situation described above, the team with the puck scores a goal and it's the fault of a player on the opposing team. Does the goal count?

Yes, if it's scored before the ref blows his whistle.

In trying to gain control of the puck, team B commits a penalty. The ref raises his hand but he does not blow his whistle. Why not?

Team A still has possession of the puck. The ref must wait until Team A loses control of the puck. Then he'll blow his whistle. If he blew his whistle immediately, he would be unfairly depriving Team A of the puck.

In the above situation, why did the goalie of Team A suddenly leave his goal unprotected and skate toward his bench?

So a sixth skater from Team A could join in the attack. It was a safe move because the second that team B gained control of the puck, the ref would blow his whistle, stop play, and charge the delayed penalty to the player from Team B.

But in the previous situation, what if a player from Team B shot the puck and it bounced off an A player and went in the goal. Would the goal count?
Yes.

Chapter 5
OFFICIALS

Is it because so much action is taking place at all times that a hockey game needs nine officials, far more than baseball, football, soccer, or basketball?

Q. *What did King Clancy, then a referee, say to a Toronto doctor who had continually criticized his officiating?*
A. *"Maybe I'm not perfect, doc, but I don't bury my mistakes like you do!"*

MEET THE OFFICIALS

How many officials are there at each hockey game?

Nine. A referee who is the "boss," two linesmen, two goal judges, an official scorer, a game timekeeper, a penalty timekeeper, and a statistician. Although not listed as an official, there is also a "video goal judge," sometimes called a "replay official."

REFEREE (THE BOSS)

How do you differentiate between the referee and the linesmen?

The ref wears a red arm band.

Who is the only official who can call a penalty that will remove a player from the ice?

The referee. However, if a linesman observes a major infraction, he can immediately inform the ref.

Which official presides over the face-off at the beginning of each period and after each score?

The referee.

Who reports to the official scorer the number of the player who made the goal?

The referee.

How many decisions (to call or not to call) does a referee make in a typical game?

About 100.

What is the toughest call for a ref?

A penalty shot.

Do referees work games in their own home town?

No. They have no home games, only road games.

Can a referee's decision be overruled?

It might be possible, but in reality, the league never changes the decision made by a ref.

Can a game be replayed if a referee makes a bad decision?

No.

Can a referee be fined by his league?

Yes.

Why would a ref be fined?

An NHL ref could be fined by the league for verbally abusing a player, making derogatory comments to the media about a player or a team, etc. In the NCAA, the ref would be suspended.

In both leagues, all refs are rated. One of the rewards to the better regarded/highest rated ref is to be assigned to playoff games, which means prestige and additional pay.

May a team appeal a ref's decision?
No.

Can a ref "call" a game (in other words, stop play) if, in his opinion, the conditions among the players are unsatisfactory?
He can call the game at any time. For example, a game can be called if the condition of the ice is considered dangerous, if players are unruly, or if he cannot control the players during or after a brawl.

If the ref is unable to continue in an NHL game, who assumes his responsibility?
He appoints a linesman, or a "standby ref" assumes the duties of the injured ref.

When a referee displays the "washout" sign, what does it mean?
The goal that was just scored does not count. To signal a "washout" the ref raises both arms to the level of his shoulders, forming a cross with his body. (See figure 15.)

What does the ref do when he loses sight of the puck?
He blows his whistle and stops play.

Q. *During his career of 800 games (from 1952 to 1971), how many shots did goalie Glen Hall face?*
A. *He faced 32,000. And that does not include the shots in practice, between periods, preseason games, etc.*

When a puck strikes a ref or linesman, is play stopped?
No, play continues. They are considered part of the rink. However, if the puck caroms off an official and goes into the goal, play is stopped. The score does not count.

Boarding

Charging

Cross-checking

Delayed calling of penalty

Elbowing

High-sticking

Holding

Interference

Hooking

Misconduct

Kneeing

Washout

Roughing

Slashing

Spearing

Tripping

Wash-out

Unsportsmanlike conduct

Icing

Slow Whistle

FIGURE 15.   Referee's signals

Can any *player speak to an official?*

No, only the team captain may speak to an official. Or, if he is not on the ice, his alternate may speak with the ref, but in either case, they may speak only about an interpretation of a rule.

What is the "referee's crease"?

This is a red semicircle with a ten-foot radius located in front of the timekeeper's seat. When the ref is inside this semicircle and is talking with another official, players are forbidden to enter the crease. (See figure 3 on page 5.)

Who checks on the competency of the referee?

Supervisors from the league's headquarters attend games to study the effectiveness of referees and linesmen.

How do referees prepare for a new season?

They attend a training camp where they run, perform calisthenics, and study rules. This is followed by officiating at three weeks of preseason exhibition games.

What does the referee do while a linesman is breaking up a fight?

He prepares to assess penalties.

In case of a dispute, whose decision is final?

The referee's.

Does the ref ever ask the opinion of a linesman if he was unable to see the play or if he was looking the other way?

In some cases.

LINESMEN

Which penalties do linesmen call?

Deliberately removing the goal post from its anchor, and too many men on the ice. But if they observe a major infraction which the ref obviously missed, they can inform the ref, who will then call the penalty.

What infractions do linesmen call?

Icing, offside, offside pass, too many men on the ice, puck leaving the rink, and when someone from either bench throws something on the ice. They also check the netting in each goal before each period.

Can a linesman call a penalty if the ref missed seeing it even though everyone else in the arena saw it?

Technically, only a ref can call a penalty in the NHL. But often a linesman who observes a penalty that the ref missed seeing will inform the ref and the ref will take action. So, indirectly, linesmen do call penalties sometimes. In the NCAA, since 1996, both the assistant ref and the linesman may call a penalty if the head ref does not see it.

Can an NHL linesman stop play to call a penalty?

He can stop play for these reasons:
1. A player is injured seriously and the ref is not aware of it.
2. Too many men are on the ice.
3. Articles are thrown on the ice.
4. A stick is thrown on the ice from the bench.

What equipment do referees and linesmen wear to protect themselves from injury?

Helmet, cup, shin guards, and hip and thigh pads.

Which official's job is it to break up fights?

The linesman's, which can get dangerous sometimes!

OTHER OFFICIALS

Who determines if the puck actually entered the goal and a score should be credited, then turns on the red light?

The goal judge. There is a goal judge behind each goal. (By the way, the puck must completely cross over the red goal line to be considered a goal. Touching the line doesn't count.)

Is the goal judge allowed to talk to the goalie?
No.

In a face-off, does the official merely drop the puck or does he toss it down?
Most of the time it is tossed down, not merely dropped.

Do goal judges switch ends during the game?
No, they stay at the same end for the entire game. But they do alternate ends of the ice every other game.

Which official credits goals and assists to the proper player?
The official scorer determines which players should receive an assist and which player should receive credit for the goal scored.

What's a "shot clock"?
Most arenas keep a running tally of "shots on goal" for both the home team and the visiting team on a separate, easily visible scoreboard called a "shot clock." Some arenas have a shot clock at each end.

What is a "shot on goal"?
A shot on goal must be within the 4' × 6' goal posts. For example, a shot wide of the goal that the goalie decides to glove or block is *not* counted as a shot on goal. Neither is a shot that hits the goal post but does not go in. But a score is a shot on goal.

Who decides if a shot will be counted as a "shot on goal"?
The official scorer makes the decision. The total shots on goal for each team is usually announced over the PA (public address system) at the end of each period.

MORE QUESTIONS ABOUT OFFICIALS

Who controls the green light behind the goal?
No one. The green light comes on and a buzzer sounds,

both automatically, when the electrically controlled time clock signals the end of a period.

Can the red light come on while the green light is on?

No. Thus if the goal judge signals a goal and the green light is already on, meaning the period has ended, the goal does not count.

During an intermission, how does a team know when to take the ice for the next period?

The referee orders that each team be notified three minutes before the start of the next period. Usually a bell is rung in each team's dressing room.

How does the fan know the reason the ref called a specific penalty?

The reason for each penalty is broadcast twice over the PA.

How do the players know when the end of a period is near?

Sixty seconds before the end of the period, the message, "There is only one minute remaining in the period," is broadcast over the PA.

What equipment do linesmen and the referee carry with them?

A whistle and a six-foot metal tape measure for measuring a possible illegal stick.

If the red light comes on but the ref does not allow the goal to be counted, must he state a reason and have this reason broadcast over the PA system?

Yes.

The referee makes almost all the hand signals during a game. In fact, the linesmen make only three hand signals. What are they?

Icing, slow whistle, and washout.

How many officials in the NHL can call a penalty?
Under normal circumstances, one. A linesman calls a
penalty only under extraordinary conditions.

Does the game clock run during a penalty shot?
No.

*When might the "video goal judge" or the "replay official"
be called in?*
He can be called in only by the ref and only on the question of whether a disputed goal should be counted. The ref
might call in the "replay official" to view his video of the
action preceding the disputed goal. Seeing a specific action
on the video might induce the ref to change his decision.
The video might answer questions like:
- Did the puck actually cross the goal line?
- Was the puck in the net before the goal frame was dis-
  lodged from the ice?
- Was the puck in the net before the period was over?
- Did someone kick or hand pass the puck into the net?
- Did the puck enter the net after it was deflected off an
  official?
- Did an attacking player high stick the puck into
  the net?
- Was the game clock correct?

*What were two of the innovations which official Fred
Waghorne made during his 50 years of officiating?*
1. To stop play, referees used to use a hand bell. He introduced the whistle.
2. On face-offs, the referee for years would carefully place
   the puck between the stick blades of the two opposing players. Waghorne suggested dropping the puck.
   Undoubtedly a lot safer!

Who was the first NHL official to work more than 1,000 games?

Between 1946 and 1965, linesman George Hayes worked 1,544 regular games, 149 playoff contests, and 11 All-Star games.

What is the name of the NHL referee who was the first to use hand signals to indicate rule infractions. This ref was elected to the Hockey Hall of Fame in 1964.

Bill Chadwick.

 *Chapter 6*
SCORING

How exciting it is to see a player score a goal! Maybe it's because, on the average, only one in ten shots is actually a goal.

Q. *What did Rocket Richard of the Montreal Canadiens do on Dec. 28, 1944, to earn him a bawling out by his coach?*
A. *It was the first crucial game of the season, against Detroit. Richard was visibly exhausted in the dressing room before the game, yet he was the one player on the team whom everyone was depending on to lead them in this vital game.*

Dick Irwin, his coach, asked the Rocket, "Why are you so tired?" Richard explained, "I moved furniture all day long. Movers are hard to come by and when you can get them, you have to take them. And today was the only day they had available."

That night, Montreal beat Detroit 9–1. Richard scored five times and assisted on three others.

Maurice "Rocket" Richard (© Bruce Bennett Studios)

HOW A PLAYER EARNS POINTS

For his personal record, how many points does a player receive for scoring a goal?
One point.

For assisting on the scoring of a goal?
One point, same as the person who scored the goal.

What is an "assist"?
Being instrumental or "assisting" in the scoring of a goal.

How many "assists" can be credited on any one goal?
A maximum of two assists on any one goal.

Who is credited with an assist?
Player(s) who passed the puck to the goal-scorer.

Is someone credited with an assist on every goal?
No. Sometimes a player scores a goal "unassisted."

Can a player receive more than one point on any goal scored?
No. He cannot receive a point for scoring a goal and another point for assisting on the scoring.

What is a "hat trick"?
When a player scores three goals in one game.

What is a "pure" hat trick?
When a player scores three *consecutive* goals.

How does a player earn scoring honors?
By getting the most points during the season.

Who is the only NHL player to average two goals per game for the entire season?
Joe Malone scored 44 goals in 20 games for the Montreal Canadiens in 1917–18. As you can see, the season was much shorter (today's regular hockey season is 82 games).

When did NHL players begin to receive credit for an assist?
The assist was initiated in the 1931–32 season.

Who is the only NHL player to score seven goals in one game?
Joe Malone scored seven goals in a 1920 game seen by only 700 fans because of the arena's –20° temperature. But not to be outdone by the sparse turnout, Joe scored six goals in the following night's game.

What was the highest salary of Joe Malone, the unparalleled star of his day?
His salary high was $1,000 a year. Because his hockey salary was so small and he needed to hold down his full-time job, he could afford to play only home games.

POINTS FOR YOUR TEAM

How many points does a team get for a win? For a tie?
Two for a win, one for a tie.

How is a team's standing within its league determined?
By the total number of points it has earned after playing other teams in its league.

If the ref stops the game (for good reason, of course, as mentioned previously) what will the score be?
Whatever the score was at the time of stopping will be the final score. However, the game must have gone at least two periods to count.

What happens when a game ends in a tie?
A five-minute overtime period is played in "sudden death" fashion: As soon as the first goal is scored, the game is over. If neither team scores during the overtime period, the game ends as a tie. The exception is a playoff game when the teams play until one of them scores, even if it takes all night (and sometimes it does).

WHAT COUNTS? WHEN IS A GOAL NOT A GOAL?

If the entire puck crosses the goal line, it's a goal unless what two things happened?
1. An attacking player kicked or threw the puck into the net
2. An attacking player is in the goalie crease and is not forcibly held there by a defender.

If the puck touches the goal line but does not go beyond it, is it a goal?

No, it is not a goal. The puck must *completely* cross the goal line.

When does a goal not count?

When the ref overrules the goal judge. Or when the ref loses sight of the puck at the last second and does not have time to blow his whistle before the puck crosses the goal line. (The ref normally blows his whistle and stops the game when he is unable to see the puck.)

If a player kicks the puck into the net, does it count?

No.

In the NHL, if you kick the puck at the goal and it deflects off an opposing player, who is not the goalie, and enters the goal, does it count as a score?

No. Neither would it count if the kicked puck deflected off the goalie. However, kicking the puck is allowed anywhere on the ice.

If the puck deflects off your skate and goes in the goal, does it count?

Yes, as long as the deflection was not intentional.

If the puck bounces off your rear end and goes in the goal, does it count?

It sure does.

If a puck shot at the goal deflects off an official and goes into the goal, does it count?

No.

If a player on the defending side accidentally puts the puck into his own goal, does it count for the opposing team?

It certainly does.

Who would get credit for scoring that goal?

The last player on the attacking side who touched the puck.

In the NCAA, if a player kicks or throws the puck into the net, does it count as a score?

No. Only the player's stick can be used to propel the puck into the net.

The puck is not in the area of the goal but an attacking player is standing inside the goalie's crease. Suddenly from far out, another attacking player's shot hits the net and a goal is scored. Does it count?

No, because the first player was inside the goalie's crease which is "off limits."

If an attacking player is pushed into the goal crease by a defending player and a goal is scored, does it count?

Yes, because the attacking player inside the crease was there involuntarily.

What if the goalie catches the puck in the air and in the act of throwing it back into play his hand holding the puck travels over the goal line inside the goal. Is it counted as a goal?

Yes.

Can a goal be scored when the green light is on?

No.

If the goal judge sees a goal scored and pushes the red light signal while the green light signalling the end of the period is already on, will the goal count?

No. And if the green light is already on, the red "scoring" light will not even operate.

An attacking player, using his stick, bats down a puck that was higher than his shoulder. The puck caroms off his stick and enters the goal. Is it a score?

No.

SHORTHANDED

What is a shorthanded goal?

One of the most exciting plays in the game, it occurs when the *shorthanded* team scores a goal.

How often does a team score when it has a power play (a man advantage)?

On average, a team will score one goal for every five times it has a man advantage.

How often do teams score when they are shorthanded?

In a typical year, one NHL team will score 20 shorthanded goals during the regular season. The team that scores the fewest will have only two for the entire season. The average team will score ten shorthanded goals, one about every eight games. The average team will play shorthanded about 350 times during the season.

SHOOTING

How are most goals scored? Where should a player aim? What are his highest "percentage" shots?

This is how most goals are scored:

1. Best chance: a low shot below the goalie's knees from ten to 25 feet out, shot on the side opposite the goalie's glove (his stick side).
2. Second best chance: a shot that's high on the goalie's stick side.
3. Third best chance: a shot five inches off the ice on the goalie's glove side.
4. Fourth best chance: a high shot on the goalie's glove side.
5. However, all goalies have some specific weakness and this weakness could change the order of 1 to 4 above.

What are the five most common types of shots on the goal?
1. A wrist shot. This is the normal and most natural shot in which the player cradles the puck on his stick blade and propels it by flexing both his bent wrists.
2. A snap shot. This is a quickly executed wrist shot, used close to the goal.
3. A slap shot. Sometimes it travels 100-plus MPH. It is often a surprise shot, and has a low scoring ratio compared to a wrist shot. When shot with a curved stick, the puck often dips before it reaches the goalie. It is difficult to aim.
4. A backhand shot. The player turns 180 degrees from his normal shooting position. Cradling the puck on the opposite side of his stick blade, he "backhands" the puck toward the goal.
5. A flip shot. This is used to hit the upper corners of the net when the player is in close or the goalie is down on the ice.

How do you execute a "slap shot"?
You lift your stick off the ice, similar to the way you would lift a golf club. Then you swing the stick down to the ice, hitting the puck as hard and fast as you can. Although it is not the most accurate shot, it is very fast.

In an average game, what are the total number of shots the entire team takes on the opponent's goal?
    20–30.

How many shots become goals?
    Under 10 percent.

Who had the most feared slap shot?
    Bobby Hull, whose slap shot traveled 120 MPH. Goalies, none of whom wore face masks at that time, were petrified at facing his blazing slap shot. Hull played for Chicago from 1957–1971, and later for the Winnipeg Jets.

MORE QUESTIONS ABOUT SCORING

What can happen when a shot on goal is deflected?
1. The puck, heading for the goal, could be deflected by a stick or a player's body and miss the goal.
2. The puck, shot wide of the goal, could deflect off a stick or a player and enter the goal for a score.
3. Or, best from the shooter's point of view, the puck could be intentionally deflected into the goal by the deft stickwork of a skillful teammate who intentionally deflects the puck. If this should happen, the goalie would hopefully be tricked by the sudden change of direction of the puck and not be able to move in time to prevent the score.

During a major penalty when the opponent's player must sit out five minutes, is there a limit to the number of goals your team can score in this five-minute period?
    No. The player with the major penalty must sit out the entire five-minute penalty regardless of the number of goals your team scores.

How often does a team score on a power play?

In 1995–96, Pittsburgh had 420 power plays and scored 109 goals. That's 26 percent, better than one goal for every four power plays. On the other side of the equation, Detroit suffered 375 penalties that same season but allowed their opponents to score only 44 goals, keeping them at bay 88 percent of the time.

If, while taking a penalty shot, the player scores on a rebound, does it count?

No.

Chapter 7
EQUIPMENT

A puck caroms off a player's shin guard. Two other players crunch each other against the boards. Slam! Bang! Those 25 pounds of protective equipment allow a player to withstand terrific abuse.

Q. *In the old days, in the minor leagues of hockey, sometimes the bus rides were 15 hours long, and often the equipment, stored in the luggage compartment under the bus, froze solid. How did the players thaw their equipment?*

A. *They placed their equipment in the shower to thaw. Then they'd put it on and play extra hard to steam out the remaining moisture.*

SKATES

Which country developed the first hockey skate?

Holland. The Dutch invented the first workable skate in the middle of the nineteenth century.

What was that first skate like?

It was a metal blade that could be strapped onto the player's regular shoe or boot.

What often went wrong with this Dutch skate?

The skate, which clamped onto the shoe, was held there by a spring. Sometimes when a puck or a stick hit the spring-loaded blade, the impact released the blade and it would fly across the ice. The ref then stopped the game while the player retrieved his blade and reattached it to his shoe.

What is the best material for a skate boot, leather or plastic?

The best skates are made of both materials. Leather, with its qualities of comfort and durability comprises most of the boot. The toe area is made of molded plastic to protect the player's foot from flying pucks and errant sticks.

Do any players go sockless under their skates?

A few. Bobby Orr and Keith Magnuson, both former all-star defensemen, say they liked the "close feel" they got when their feet were in direct contact with their skate boots. Eric Lindros of the Philadelphia Flyers also wears no socks.

How often does a player have his skates sharpened?

Some players have them sharpened once a week, some before each game, and some have them sharpened between periods!

How do you test your skates to determine if they are sharp?

Rub your fingernail on the edge of the blade. You should get shavings from your nail if the blade is sharp.

What is "hollow ground" sharpening?

It's a professional method of sharpening in which the blade is slightly "U" shaped, leaving two edges and a "hollow" middle.

Do blades have an arc or are they flat?

All blades have an arc. The degree of the arc depends on personal preference and the position which the player plays. A large flat area (large arc) makes the skate faster because more of its blade is on the ice. But the longer the flat area, the more difficult it is to turn, cut, stop, and dodge. Defensemen usually have a longer flat area than forwards.

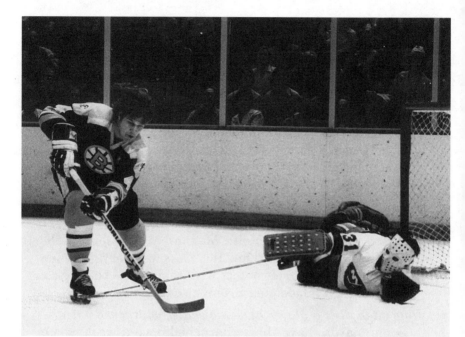

Bobby Orr attempts to put one past Billy Smith. (© Mel DiGiacomo/BBS)

How long do a player's skates last?

The bigger the player, the faster he wears out his skates. Conversely, the faster and lighter player's skates last longer. In the NHL, the average player wears out at least two pair of skates each season; in the NCAA, one pair each season.

Must all skates have protective heel equipment?

Yes.

When was the first molded plastic skate widely used?

In 1958. The new plastic boot gave the players more protection and more support.

STICKS

What are hockey sticks made of?
Aluminum (shafts), wood, fiberglass, and glue.

Why do players wrap the blade of their stick with black tape?
To hide the puck, making it difficult for the goalie to see the puck as it flies toward him. Also, because tape wrapped around the blade of the stick cushions the puck, players believe a taped blade increases their control over the puck.

How many sticks does a player use?
Generally, one stick for each game and one for every two practice sessions. The actual amount depends upon several factors including:
1. The position he plays.
2. The amount of ice time he receives during a game.
3. The number of practices during a week.
4. The style of hockey he plays.
5. How hard he shoots.
6. The quality of the stick; the more fiberglass it contains, the longer it will last.

What is the "lie" of a stick?
It is the angle or "degree of uprightness" between the blade and the shaft. Every stick has a lie. It ranges from three to eight, the higher the number the more vertical the stick. The player's style of skating is the major determining factor in which lie he prefers. For example, a player who likes to carry the puck way out in front of him would have a stick with a lower lie than a player who likes to carry the puck in close to him. (See figure 16.)

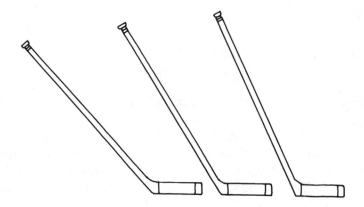

FIGURE 16.   Sticks and their lies. A stick's lie is determined by its angle of the blade on the ice, and depends on a player's preference. Some players prefer to keep the puck close to them while skating, while others prefer to carry the puck farther in front of them.

How should a player determine what lie is best for him?

He should try a variety of stick lies when he is on his skates, not in his shoes. The skates add about three inches to his height and change the angle (the lie).

Are the blades of most hockey sticks curved?

Yes. Developed in the 1960s, the curved blade adds about 15 MPH to the velocity of the player's shot. The curved blade also makes the puck sink as it approaches the goalie. Goalies probably wish the curved stick was never invented!

What is the maximum curvature allowed for a stick?

Maximum curvature is 1/2 inch from the tip of the stick to the heel.

What happens when a team requests a referee to stop the game and measure a stick on the opposing team, believing it to be illegal?

The NHL both penalizes and fines a player using an illegal stick. In the NCAA, a player using an illegal stick is assessed both a minor penalty and a misconduct penalty.

But what if the stick in question really is legal?

In the NCAA, if the stick is legal, the team that requests the examination is penalized for delaying the game. In the NHL, not only is the "questioning" team penalized but it is also fined.

Are there sticks designed for both right-sided and left-sided shooters?

Yes. A "lefty" stick is curved just the opposite from a "righty" stick. Some sticks are neutral: the blade is straight and has no curve or lean.

Why do players wind a knob of black tape at the "handle" end of their stick?

To prevent their top hand from sliding off the end of the stick when they shoot or stickhandle. The knob also makes it easier for them to pick up their stick when it's knocked out of their hands and is lying on the ice.

When did aluminum-shaft sticks become popular?

The NHL approved them in December 1981.

PUCKS

How many pucks are used in an average game?

Twelve to fifteen.

Why are pucks frozen before every game?

So they can be passed accurately without bouncing, and so they will move faster across the ice.

Has the puck always been black?

Yes, except for a postseason trial of 23 games in 1959 when an orange puck was substituted. But the players complained (probably because it was easier for goalies to see this brighter puck), and that was the end of the experiment.

What is the puck made of?
Hard vulcanized rubber.

How hard is it?
Very hard.

How lethal a weapon is a puck?
Many players have lost teeth and have required facial stitches because they were hit by a puck. Also, a puck flying into the stands can be devastating.

What words are printed on a puck?
No words. On one side is the NHL logo and on the other side is the logo of the home team.

Where are "spare" pucks kept during a game?
They're contained in a brine and ice solution, to keep them at a temperature below freezing.

Who developed the modern puck, setting its weight, diameter, thickness, color, etc?
Art Ross, former coach and general manager of the Boston Bruins. The puck has remained unchanged throughout much of the twentieth century.

GOALIE'S SPECIAL EQUIPMENT

What protective equipment does a goalie wear?
Thick arm and shoulder pads, a heavy chest protector, leg pads that cover his instep, a glove to block with, another glove to catch the puck, a helmet, and a mask. (See figure 6 on page 7.)

What are two types of gloves that a goalie wears?
One is a "blocker" that he wears on his stick hand to ward off shots. The other is a "trapper," similar to a first baseman's glove, which he uses to catch the puck in the air.

How do a goalie's skates differ from those worn by the other players?

The blade has a very flat arc and the skate is designed so that a puck cannot slide between the boot and the blade. The boot has special toe and ankle protectors.

How did goalie Clint Benedict attempt in vain to protect his nose from being broken?

On Feb. 20, 1930, he entered the game wearing a leather face protector that covered his nose and mouth. But when it became dislodged in a goal-mouth scramble and he ended up with another broken nose, he retired from that game, the season, and his hockey career.

Who popularized the wearing of the goaltender's mask?

Although Clint Benedict (1917 to 1930) wore a makeshift leather "mask" in 1930 to protect his oft-broken nose, it was Jacques Plante's (1952 to 1973) perseverance with his own mask that led the way for all goalies to adopt the mask.

Who were the last NHL goalies to hold out against wearing a mask?

Gump Worsley (who played from 1952 to 1974) did not don a mask until he joined the Buffalo Sabres, his last season in the NHL. He estimated he had 250 facial stitches by that time. Andy Brown of Detroit (1971 to 1974) was the other holdout.

What was special about the goalie mask worn by Gerry Cheevers of the Bruins (1961 to 1980)?

It was decorated with stitches painted on the mask to show what his face would have looked like had he not worn a mask.

What are two major innovations in goaltending equipment made in the 1940s, and what two goaltenders devised these innovations?

Frank Brimsek, "Mr. Zero" of the Bruins (1938 to 1950), developed the "blocker" glove that enabled him to repel

Gerry Cheevers and his "stitches mask" (© M. DiGiacomo/BBS)

shots with his stick hand. In 1948 Emile "Cat" Francis (1946 to 1952) introduced a baseball first baseman's type glove which he used expertly on his puck-catching hand.

HELMETS AND FACEGUARDS

Is wearing a helmet mandatory?
It is required by the NHL, NCAA, US amateur leagues, high schools, and Canadian youth hockey. Mandatory helmet use was brought about by the death of Bill Masterson in 1968, who fell to the ice and never recovered from the head trauma. This, the NHL's first fatality, led to adoption of the helmet rule.

Does the NCAA require all players to wear a faceguard?
Yes, complete with chin strap.

How about mouth guards? Are they required?
In the NCAA, yes.

In the NHL, most forwards and defensemen wear mouth protectors, but some goalies refuse to do so. Why?
Because they must constantly shout directions to their teammates and a mouthguard would inhibit this.

College players wear faceguards and helmets. Why don't all pro players protect themselves in the same manner?
Some players who refuse to wear a face guard say it cuts down on their vision and hampers their movements.

How many types of face protectors are there?
Two. Clear plastic and wire cages.

When did players start to wear helmets?
In 1959–60, four players wore helmets: Vic Stasiuk and Charlie Burns of Boston, Warren Godfrey of Detroit, and Camille Henry of New York.

Why is the toothless hockey player becoming extinct?

Largely because of the face protector and the mouthpiece that boxers have worn for decades, which protects teeth and prevents a player from biting his tongue.

COST OF EQUIPMENT

Here is the equipment that one NCAA Division I college provides each player, and the cost of each piece. The college team has 20 players, including two goalies whose special equipment is not listed here. (Costs were accurate at the time this was written.)

1. Travel bag	$ 30.00	
2. Skates	225.00	
3. Shin pads	74.00	
4. Pants	83.00	
5. Elbow pads	38.00	
6. Gloves	90.00	
7. Helmet	38.50	
8. Faceguard	27.00	
9. Practice jersey	10.00	
10. Practice socks	10.00	
11. Shoulder pads	85.00	(to $140)
12. Sticks (doz.)	230.00	(custom stick)
13. Garter belt	5.00	
14. Suspenders	5.50	
15. Tape	1.50	
16. Laces	2.00	

The cost of equipping a 20-man team is $25,000.

OTHER QUESTIONS ABOUT EQUIPMENT

What are some examples of dangerous or unlawful equipment?

1. Elbow pads with no exterior sponge rubber.
2. Gloves cut to reveal the bare hand.
3. Speed skates and fancy skates.
4. Sticks with excessive curvature in the blade, sharp ends, length too long, and blade too high
5. Certain face shields and masks with high potential for injury (ones not shatterproof).

Must all equipment be worn under clothing?
Yes, except gloves, helmet, mask, and the goalie's pads.

What does a player use a garter for?
To hold up his heavy stockings.

How does a player break in a new pair of stiff gloves?
Often by immersing them in water and then wearing them in practice sessions.

What have been the greatest improvements in protective clothing in the last 20 years?
The face mask and helmet.

How much does a player's equipment weigh?
From 25 to 27 pounds. Most of this weight is in shoulder pads, pants, shin pads, and skates. A goalie's equipment weighs about ten pounds more.

Who is credited with inventing the first hockey goal net?
W. A. Hewitt, secretary of the Ontario Hockey Association, invented the first goal net when, to end disputes on whether the puck had actually entered the goal, he draped a fish net over the goal posts.

When did the player's name first appear on the back of his sweater?
It was allowed beginning in 1970 and became mandatory in 1977.

How did Harold Bullard, the owner of the Toronto Maple Leafs, attempt to circumvent the rule that his players must wear their name on the back of their sweater?

Bullard figured that if fans could read the names of the players on their sweaters, then they would not buy a program to identify the players, and he'd lose money. So, on their blue sweaters, he placed blue letters, making the names unreadable. But he changed his tune and by the next game each Toronto player had a readable name on the back of his sweater.

When was the green light instituted behind each goal?

In 1938. When the green light is on, signaling the end of the period, it is electrically impossible for the red light to come on. Thus a goal cannot be scored once time runs out.

The ice surface inside the goal and a semicircle outside the goal is colored blue. Why?

To make it easier for both skaters and officials to determine when players are in this area when they should not be.

How many manufacturers of hockey equipment are there?

In addition to numerous stick producers, there are at least 17 firms in the US and Canada that manufacture gloves, skates, pads, etc.

What color uniforms do NHL teams wear at home?

Home teams wear light colored uniforms. Visiting team players wear dark uniforms.

"I can't skate well because I have weak ankles." Is this a realistic argument?

Either you have improperly fitted skates or your skates are not laced correctly. (Unless of course, you have an actual physical disability.)

Chapter 8
FACILITIES

A new ice surface is laid in less than ten minutes. Amazing!

Q. *What NHL goalie "flashed" the length of the ice?*
A. *Gilles Gratton of the New York Rangers planned to do it in the Maple Leaf Gardens on the last game of the season. As a "warmup" one day in practice, when the session happened to be covered by a reporter, Gilles streaked down the ice dressed only in his skates, socks, mask, and jockstrap. He did it because "I was bored with hockey." (However, when that last game of the season finally came around, he disappointed his teammates, chickened out, and never did perform as promised.)*

When were glass partitions above the boards introduced and why?
Before the 1960–61 season in the Montreal Forum. It had been the scene of an excessive number of fan injuries from sticks and pucks, and protective glass was installed above the boards.

Name five functions of the plexiglass that surrounds the rink.
1. Protects the fans from flying pucks.
2. Soundproofs the players against the noise of the fans.

3. Prevents rowdy fans from littering the ice.
4. Helps to keep the puck in play.
5. Prevents the players from being checked into the first row of fans.

How often does this plexiglass break?
The average arena experiences two to five breaks each season. Causes of breaks:

1. Temperature. The colder the arena, the more breaks.
2. Each pane of glass has a small air bubble that when hit by a player, stick, or puck, causes the glass to break. The more accessible the bubble, the more breaks.

Most rinks in North America measure 200 feet long and 85 feet wide. What is the size of rinks in Europe?
Most are 200 feet long and 100 feet wide.

How long does it take to freeze the ice the first time? Is it there all season? What happens when a basketball court is laid over the ice?
To make ice for the first time in a season takes at least 24 hours, most often two to five days. Some rinks keep the ice all year round. There are 4 miles of pipe under the rink. When a basketball court is laid on the ice, first a layer of insulation (usually homosote) is laid over the ice. Sometimes a layer of plywood is laid directly over the ice. If plywood is used, the ice must be scraped and shaved after the plywood is removed to make sure that no debris remains that could be dangerous to the hockey players.

How thick is the ice in a hockey rink?
From 2.5–3.5 inches.

What is "slow" ice?
Ice that has a soft surface; sometimes you can even see water reflected on its surface. The puck travels slower on such ice and players cannot skate as fast. The entire game

is slower and more frustrating for the players who are used to fast, hard ice.

What is a "Zamboni"?

A Zamboni is a Jeep-like vehicle that makes ice. It is named after its manufacturer. There are other kinds of resurfacing machines, too. All rinks have at least one Zamboni or another expensive resurfacing machine.

Before the invention of the Zamboni ice-making machine, how long did it take to lay down a fresh sheet of ice?

What the Zamboni does in ten minutes with one man, used to require six men and 90 minutes.

How does the Zamboni make new ice?

Before the game and after each period, the Zamboni shaves the ice. How much it shaves off depends upon the ice condition and the temperature inside the arena. A rotary blade in the rear of the machine accumulates the shaved ice and by belt transfers it to a hollow cavity inside the Zamboni. The machine then pumps warm water on the ice and smooths it with the cloth that trails behind. The pipes beneath the surface then immediately freeze the smooth warmed water into a sheet of new, fast ice.

How many Zamboni machines are there? What kind of engines do they have?

There are about 5,000 and they are powered by Volkswagen engines.

Chapter 9

PLAYERS

What's it take to play hockey? What does a coach look for in a player?

Several years ago, Bobby Hull of the Chicago Black-hawks was timed electronically.
Q. *What was his skating speed?*
A. *29.2 MPH*
Q. *How fast was his slapshot?*
A. *119.5 MPH*

SKILLS

What physical capabilities must a player combine?
1. The ruggedness of a football player.
2. The finesse of a baseball player.
3. The endurance of a long distance runner.
4. The strength of a weight lifter.
5. The coordination of a golfer.
6. The agility of a figure skater.

What skills do most coaches seek in a hockey player?
This is what they look for and in this order.
1. Skating ability.

Bobby Hull playing here for the Winnipeg Jets. (© Bruce Bennett Studios)

2. Stickhandling
3. Position play.
4. Playmaking ability.
5. Scoring ability.
6. Physical ruggedness.

What is "split vision"? Must all players possess it?

Split vision is the ability to see both the puck on your stick (on the ice), and at the same time see an opponent (in front of you) who is about to crash into you, or a fellow player who is in position for a pass. Split vision is a requisite for a hockey player. You can't play the game without it.

If a player is not skilled enough to make any of the three forward lines, what qualities must he have to be a team member?

In addition to being a good player, he must be dedicated and unselfish, and be ready at all times. Sulking is out; he must think always of the team's best interest. (A team will have three or four forward lines, a line made up of a left and right wing and a center. The first line is made up of the best scorers, while the last lines are more physical, concentrating on defense.)

Why is a beginning player taught to skate with his head up, not down?

A player who skates with his head down runs the danger of having it separated from his body by the first opponent who confronts him.

CAPTAINS

How can you recognize the team captain?

He wears a large "C" on his jersey.

Can a goalie ever be the team captain?

Not in the NHL; it's OK in the NCAA.

How many alternate captains are there and how do you recognize them?
There are a maximum of two and each wears a large "A" on the front of his jersey.

What subjects are the captain or the alternate captains allowed to discuss with the ref?
The only subject they can discuss must be an "interpretation of the rules."

Is a complaint *about a penalty to be construed as "interpretation of the rules" and a fit subject for discussion?*
No.

If the team captain comes off the bench to complain to the referee, what happens?
He will receive a misconduct penalty plus a minor penalty. This holds true for *any* player who comes off the bench to complain.

Does a coach or manager ever serve as team captain?
No.

While reading the following sections about centers, wings, and defensemen, it's important to remember that because hockey is the fastest team sport, its players must constantly "read and react" to the situation at that moment. Their roles are fluid and their responsibilities change from second to second.

THE CENTER

Which forward player is usually involved in the face-off?
The center.

What does a center try to do on offense?
1. He works up and down the middle of the ice.

2. Leads his team's attack by bringing the puck up the ice.
3. Sets up plays.
4. Passes the puck to his two wing men.
5. Tries to aim the play at the opponent's goal.
6. Although he usually faces off and follows the puck wherever it goes, this depends on the system (or the game plan) that the team is using.
7. Positions himself effectively to receive a pass from his defensemen.

What is the center's job on defense?
1. He forechecks the puck carrier.
2. Tries to keep the play and the puck in the opponent's defending zone.
3. Harasses the puck carrier.
4. Tries to break up plays.
5. Keeps circling in the neutral zone to pick up an opposing player.
6. Prevents the opposing winger from making a rink-wide pass.
7. Makes sure that his team is never outnumbered in their defending zone.
8. But his primary job on defense is to cover the slot in his own defending zone.

What is a center's greatest asset?
Speed and strength are important, but if he reads the play wrong, his other skills and talents might be useless. His greatest asset is the same as that of all the other players: the ability to read a situation and react properly to it.

Why does the center need incredible stamina?
He's the only player on the ice who must skate continually from one end to the other end of the rink.

WINGS

Must a left wing shoot from the left side?

Not necessarily. Rocket Richard of the Canadiens shot from the left side but was the league's most devastating *right* wing.

Does the left wing always play on the left side of the rink?

No. Sometimes he's in the middle, and sometimes on the right side of the rink. In the eye of the player, the rink has three "alleys," a left alley, a center alley, and a right alley. As long as each of these three alleys is occupied by one of the three forwards, the team will have carried out a successful strategy. (The above goes for the right wing, too.)

What is the job of each wing on offense?
1. To skate down the side of the rink.
2. Pass the puck back and forth to the center.
3. Position himself for a shot on the goal.
4. Score goals.
5. Dig the puck out from the corners and pass it to a teammate.
6. When the opponents have possession of the puck in a corner of their own defending zone, a wing should be the first player on his team to skate to that corner. His aim is to separate the opposing player from the puck. When he has dislodged the puck from the opponent, he will depend upon his center or other wing to take possession of the loose puck.

What's the job of a wing on defense?
1. To cover the opponent's wing.
2. Try to break up the play.
3. Guard the points and prevent opponents from getting in position at either point.

4. Eliminate the opponent's defensemen from the play.
5. Cover the opposing defensemen at the blue line.
6. Be open for an outlet pass from one of his own team.
7. On defense, the wing positions himself along the boards, 10–20 feet behind the blue line.

DEFENSE

What do defensemen do on offense?
1. Carry the puck up the ice or pass it to their forwards.
2. Follow the play into the opponent's defending zone.
3. Help keep the puck within their team's attacking zone, not allowing the puck to cross the blue line into the neutral zone.
4. If he is unable to shoot or pass the puck without hitting an opposing player (who might intercept the puck), he shoots the puck into the corner.
5. Maintain control and set up plays during a "power play."

What's the job of a defenseman while he's playing defense?
1. Stop the incoming play at his own blue line.
2. Block shots.
3. Clear the puck when it's in front of his goal.
4. Watch the opposing forwards; prevent them from scoring.
5. Make the transitional play from defense to offense.

Does the left defenseman always play on the left side of the rink?

Hockey is a game where reaction is very important. Often the left defenseman will cross over to the right side of the rink to assist in a play. (The same pertains to right defensemen.) There is really little difference between a left defenseman and a right defenseman, except on face-offs, when each one plays on his designated side.

CHECKING

Why is there so much physical contact in hockey?

It has *always* been a major aspect of the game. Through a well-timed check, a player can break up a play by taking out an opposing skater who has possession of the puck. The check could not only stop the opposing skater but it might also result in dislodging the puck from his control. This, in turn, could result in regaining possession of the puck. In addition, physical contact can help your team intimidate the opposition, making them act tentatively and ineffectively. When used correctly, physical contact can be an important part of a team's strategy.

Can a player check an opposing player who is in possession of the puck anywhere on the rink?

Yes.

What are the two major methods of confronting an opponent who has the puck?

Your intent is to cause him to lose control of the puck. You can try to do this by:

1. Going after the *puck* with your stick, and trying to take it away from him.
2. Going after his *body,* holding him (legally) and forcing him to lose control of the puck.

When are the best times to bodycheck your opponent?

When he's passing or receiving the puck. His guard is down and most of his attention is on the puck. Or when he's carrying the puck with his head down and doesn't see you.

What's the worst time to bodycheck?

When you are the last defense between the puck carrier and the goal. If you miss your bodycheck, your opponent will probably have a clear path to your goal.

In bodychecking, is it more advisable to aim for the body or for the puck?

Go for the body. It's easier to make contact with the body than to try to take away the puck. The body is a larger target.

Although the defending player keeps his eyes on the chest of the puck carrier, he searches for the puck with his peripheral vision. He knows that if the puck carrier's hands are free, he is still capable of passing the puck to a teammate.

What are legitimate bodychecks?

1. The *shoulder check* is the most common check. It generally is used to check an opponent into and against the boards. The player executing the check drives his shoulder and hip into his opponent's body.
2. The *hip check* is more difficult to execute but even a grazing hip check may be sufficient to make the puck carrier lose control of the puck.
3. The *board check.* The purpose is to squeeze your opponent against the boards so he'll either lose the puck or be forced into a bad angle for passing or shooting at your goal.
4. Probably the most devastating is the *open ice check,* often called the "face-to-face" check.

ON AND OFF THE ICE

How does a player on the bench know when to relieve the player he usually replaces?

He watches only that player whose place he will take. He waits and watches for a signal that the skater he will replace is ready to come off the ice. And, of course, he listens to his coach's orders to change.

Does a team change players "on the fly" when it is on defense or on offense?

Only when their team is on offense. If they made a change while they were on defense, they would leave their defensemen and goalie unprotected.

When a player breaks his stick and rushes to the bench to get a replacement stick, how does he know he will be handed a duplicate and not a stick that will not fit him?

Each team has an equipment person on the bench whose job is to have at all times an exact replacement stick immediately ready for each player.

Who will pick up the broken stick from the ice? Will play stop?

Play will not be stopped because of a broken stick lying on the ice. When play does stop, one of the officials will pick up the broken stick.

PASSING

List seven ways a player may pass the puck to a teammate, depending upon the circumstances at the time.
1. Sweep pass.
2. Snap pass.
3. Flip pass.
4. Lift pass.
5. Clearing pass.
6. Drop pass.
7. Board pass.

What's a "flip" pass?

A pass that is lifted off the ice into the air so it will be difficult for an opposing player to intercept it. It's a normal pass except it flies through the air instead of along the ice. You use a flip pass when you're making a long pass and don't want it intercepted.

What's a "drop" pass?

You're entering the attacking zone with the puck in your possession and you encounter an opponent. You can't go through him and you can't go around him. So you stop the puck, keep on skating but leave the puck for a teammate who is immediately behind you. He then swoops up the loose puck and skates around the surprised opposing player. The drop pass works well for those players who have eyes in the back of their head and ESP with their teammates. But sometimes you can fool your own teammate who is not expecting you to execute a "drop" pass. This may cause your team to lose possession of the puck.

What's a "suicide pass"?

When the receiver of a pass is forced to turn his head to receive a pass. He becomes a sitting duck for a hard check from an opponent. Ouch!

BROKEN STICKS AND PLAYERS

If a player is injured, cannot continue to play, and is unable to skate to his bench, does play stop?

No, not until his team secures possession of the puck. If his team has possession of the puck and is in position to score, play continues. But if it is apparent that the injury is *serious,* the ref or a linesman can stop play immediately.

Can a player who breaks his stick obtain another stick by having someone bring it to him?

No. He must skate to his bench and get his own stick. However, if a goalie loses or breaks his stick, a teammate on the ice at that time will give the goalie his own stick, even though it is not a goalie stick.

What are the two most common injuries among hockey players?

A pulled groin and a muscle pull.

MORE QUESTIONS ABOUT PLAYERS

Once a coach submits his lineup before the game, can he add to it if he's forgotten a player?

No, and that forgotten player cannot participate in the game.

How many offensive lines does a team have?

Three, sometimes four.

How many defensemen does a team usually have?

Five or six.

Can a player legally kick the puck?

Yes. For a player who has lost his stick, this might be all he can do until he gets a new one or regains control of his old one. In fact, you can play the entire game without a stick and merely kick it. But you wouldn't be a very potent force, would you!

Do many left-shooting players also shoot from their right side? And vice versa?

No. Switch hitters might be common in baseball, but there have been mighty few hockey players who could shoot from both sides of their body. Of this rare breed, Gordie Howe was the most outstanding.

Is hockey the only game in which players are substituted at any time without waiting for play to stop?

Yes.

How difficult is it for a player to make a backhand shot using a stick with a curved blade?

Although it's certainly more difficult to direct a shot accurately with a curved blade than with a straight blade, many players have mastered the curved-blade-backhand shot. Their secret is the same as for many other things in life: practice, practice, practice.

Can a team change players at any time it wishes, even during play?

Yes. But, once the team is lined up for a face-off, the referee holds up his hand and, after that, the team cannot change players.

In college hockey, before the season begins, the home team can select which goal it will defend for periods one and three throughout the season, and also which players bench it wants. True or false?

Both are true and each selection gives the home team an advantage. In selecting the same goal to defend each period during the entire season, the home team becomes even more familiar with its home rink. It will normally select the bench nearest the penalty box so that any penalized player will have quicker access to the home team's bench. College officials will also designate the side of the arena on which the home team's bench is located as "the home side" so that the team will benefit from the cheering of the home team fans.

Q. *In pregame warmups, what did Bobby Hull (who played from 1957 to 1980) and his brother Dennis (1964 to 1978) like to do with their new curved sticks?*
A. *During pregame practice, their least favorite goal judge had a habit of holding a bottle of soda in his hand. The two Hull brothers, who both played for Chicago, delighted in shooting the puck at the plexiglass directly in front of his face, watching him jump with fright and spill his drink all over himself.*

How many calories does a player burn up during one game?
About 800.

How many pounds will he lose?
About five.

Q. *Left winger "Toe" Blake, the Canadiens' notorious "bad man," won the Lady Byng trophy (for gentlemanly play) in 1946, the first year he was teamed up on the same line with right wing Rocket Richard. How did he explain his sudden turnaround from bad man to gentleman?*
A. *"All night long I tried to keep up with the Flying Frenchman. I was always too pooped to fight!" he said.*

Why do players climb over the boards to get to and from their bench? Why don't they use the door?
Hockey is a game of speed. Players want to get on the ice *quickly.* The fastest way is to jump over the boards.

Can a player not in uniform at the beginning of the game play during that game?
No.

Do any players wear eyeglasses?
Not during the game. But several wear contact lenses.

How about hearing aids?
Yes, some players wear hearing aids.

Do hockey players have a higher threshold of pain than other athletes?
Some hockey players continue to play with great pain, but that is true in all sports. The ability to play with pain is an individual trait, and is not confined to players of any specific sport.

Maurice "Rocket" Richard and Edgar Laprade battle it out on the ice.
(© Bruce Bennett Studios)

What is the average number of years of a professional playing in the NHL?
Five to seven years according to Simon Fraser University of Vancouver, BC.

How long a shift does a defenseman usually have?
About 120 seconds on the clock.

How many players on a NHL team?
Eighteen players and two goalies.

How many on a college team?
Eighteen players and a maximum of three goalies.

What's the size and age of the typical NHL player?
Six feet tall, 190 pounds, and 26 years old.

When I attend a hockey game, what should I look at?
First of all, don't watch the puck all the time. Try this: Select one player and watch everything he does. Does he rove all over the rink? Or does he play his position tightly? Does he like to hit, or does he shy away from hitting? Does he pass the puck right away or does he carry it? Which way does he skate the best, clockwise or counterclockwise?

Q. *What's the record for the most brothers involved in one single NHL game?*

A. *Six brothers, all named Sutter. In one game, when the St. Louis Blues played the Chicago Black-hawks, this is how each of the six brothers was involved:*

1. Brian as Blues head coach
2. Darryl as associate coach, Chicago
3. Rich as Blues player (Rich and Ron are twins)
4. Ron as Blues player
5. Duane as Chicago scout
6. Brent as Chicago player

In the NCAA on the day of a game, what's the schedule of a typical player?
1. He does his "own thing" to get himself mentally prepared.
2. Eats a healthy breakfast.
3. Attends all his classes so nothing academically is nagging him.
4. Eats a training meal about five hours before the game.

5. Relaxes by taking a nap or just lounging around.
6. Does nothing that might distract him from thinking about how he wants to play tonight's game: i.e., no calls home and no calls to his girlfriend.

What are hockey players advised to eat and drink?
1. Everything that could be of some use to the body.
2. Plenty of vegetables, meats, and carbohydrate-rich foods.
3. Something from all four food groups.
4. Orange juice and milk.

What should players avoid?
1. Junk food, soda pop, and alcohol.
2. On game day, avoid milk. It increases and quickens lactic acid buildup, which leads to muscle fatigue.

How important is height and weight in a hockey player?
There are obvious advantages to being big: You are more intimidating, have more weight to throw around, and have a longer reach. The position a skater plays and his style of play determine how important it is to be 220 pounds instead of 170, or 6′4″ instead of 5′9″. (Wayne Gretzky is 6′, 170 lbs.) Of great importance is a player's strength, stamina, drive, balance, skill, and intellect. "It's not the size of the dog in the fight; it's the size of the fight in the dog."

How dangerous is it for a player to attempt to smother an opponent's shot with his body?
It can be fatal; a Manchester, New Hampshire, high school player died during the 1990–91 season blocking a shot with his body. To minimize injury to his body, the player must be sure to let only padded parts of his body hit the ice. Blocking should not be attempted inside the hash marks because an unsuccessful blocking might deflect the puck right past your own goalie and into the net. It goes without saying that no one except the goalie should attempt

to smother the puck inside the crease. If anyone but the goalie falls on the puck within the crease, the other team will be awarded a penalty shot.

Do the players on each line play the same amount of minutes during a game or do the players on the better lines get to play more minutes?

Those players who are on "special teams," such as penalty-killing teams and power-play teams, get to play a little more than those who do not play on special teams.

Chapter 10
GOALIES

How would *you* like to face a 250-pounder skating towards you at 25 MPH, shooting a hard rubber disc over 100 MPH right at you?

Q. *How many goaltenders have scored a goal in the entire history of the American Hockey League?*
A. *Only two, and the score that best illustrates this fact took place in March of 1992. It happened like this: The Springfield Indians were leading the Rochester Americans 3–2 late in the game when Rochester pulled its goalie for an extra attacker. Paul Cohen, the Springfield goalie, deflected a Rochester shot. The puck fell to the ice in front of him, and with his big stick, he shot the puck the length of the ice right into the unprotected Rochester goal.*

EQUIPMENT

How often do goalies sharpen their skates?
Some never sharpen their skates all season long, believing that sharp blades grab the ice and prevent them from sliding easily.

Why do most goalies have their own water bottle and place it on top of the net?

A goalie perspires a great deal during the game from the weight of his equipment, the stress he is under, and the great activity of his position. Besides, unlike the other players, he has no access to water during the entire period.

CHECKING

Is it legal to check the goalie when he's in his crease?

No, that's *his* territory. In fact, many who venture into the goal crease have been known to receive a whack from the goalie's stick.

In the NHL, is the goalie "fair game" and open to being checked if he's outside the crease?

No. When an opposing player makes unnecessary contact with the goalie, that player is penalized, even if the goalie was *behind* his net. A penalty will be called for interference, usually a two-minute minor.

INJURIES

When a goalie is injured, does play stop?

No, and no time is allowed for the injured goalie to get repaired. He either continues to play or a substitute goalie is sent in. However, if it's obvious that the injury is serious, an official may stop play immediately.

If a goalie is replaced by another goalie because of an injury, is the replacement goalie given a warmup period?

No. However, the team could use its only timeout for this purpose if it wished.

PENALTIES AND ICING

Can the goalie throw the puck toward the opponent's goal?
No. But he can *shoot* it toward the other goal.

What if the goalie deliberately drops the puck inside his pads or onto the top or back of the net?
He gets a two-minute minor penalty for delaying the game.

Neither team is shorthanded. A player on your team shoots the puck over the red line and blue line. If it carries over the goal line, the ref will call icing. But my goalie intercepts the puck and prevents it from crossing the goal line. Will the ref call icing?
No.

Why would the goalie want to prevent an icing call by the referee?
1. His team may have the momentum and he does not want to interrupt that momentum.
2. He may want to surprise the other team, catching it off guard.

If a goalie is penalized, must he retire to the penalty box and serve his time like any other player?
No, but a player from his team who was on the ice when the penalty occurred must serve the penalty for the goalie.

When a team pulls its goalie temporarily for the purpose of putting a sixth skater on the ice, must the goalie be seated on the bench before the sixth skater can leave the bench and join the game?
No, the sixth skater can take the ice when the goalie gets within five feet of the bench (NHL), or when the goalie touches the boards on the way off the ice (NCAA).

Chapter 11
STRATEGY

The ferocious pace of hockey makes the carefully rehearsed X and O plays of some other sports impossible. But there *is* strategy on the ice, and the players are developing it right in front of your eyes.

PASSING

What's a "feed"?
Passing the puck to another player.

What is "headmanning" the puck?
Passing the puck up the ice to a teammate rather than carrying it up yourself. The puck travels much faster by being *passed* than by being carried. In an attack, you would *pass* the puck up the ice to your team's head man.

A "blind pass," passing the puck without looking for a receiver, is a serious mistake. What are some of the other things you could do instead of passing blind?
  1. Stickhandle for a better position.
  2. Hold the puck as long as you can until you observe one of your teammates open.

What damage could a blind pass lead to?
  1. Loss of control of the puck.
  2. A breakaway for an opponent.
  3. A missed opportunity to pass to a teammate.
  4. A score by your opponent.

What are the basic strategies on offense?
1. To control the puck in the attacking zone.
2. To pass the puck around so quickly that your opponents will be scrambling hard to maintain their coverage and their defensive position and:
   a. their defense will break down
   b. an offensive opportunity will open up for your team

If there is one *unbreakable rule in the game of hockey, what is it?*

Don't ever carry the puck close to the front of your own net. If you ever lose control of the puck in front of your net, your opponent has a golden opportunity to score because there probably will be no one between him and your goalie. If you ever do carry the puck in front of your net and you *do* lose it and a score *does* result, you're going to feel very, very foolish!

Where are the "points" and who uses them?

The "points" are unmarked locations on the ice about five feet from the boards and inside your opponent's blue line within the attacking zone. Defensemen, located at the points, often shoot on the goal from this location. However, when passing the puck to a player stationed at one of the points, you must be careful that there is no opposing player close by who might intercept the pass and make a break for your own goal.

CHECKING

What is forechecking?

Forechecking is the defensive maneuver a team makes when it is still in the attacking zone and the opponents have just gained control of the puck. The purpose of forechecking is to pin your opponents in their own end of the ice and

Bruce Gardiner of the Ottawa Senators (© OSHC/Sportsfocus)

make it difficult for them to initiate an attack. Effective forechecking gives your defense time to organize itself.

Usually your center will try to harass the puck carrier. If the puck carrier tries to skate to his left to avoid your center, your right wing will move in and double team him. If the puck carrier tries to go the other way, your center and *left* wing will gang up on him. But only two of your men (never three) will forecheck at any one time. (Sending three men leaves you vulnerable to attack, as only two men will be playing defense.)

Another aim of forechecking is to steal the puck away from the opposition and gain control of the puck.

What is backchecking?

This is the activity of forwards when they play *defense*. They skate side by side with their attacking counterpart: your left wing with the opponent's right wing, your right wing with their left wing. Among the purposes of the backchecking forwards is to intercept a pass and prevent a shot on your goal.

What's an "open ice" body check?

When, in full control of your actions, you make solid contact with your opponent in an area not close to the boards.

What's "riding your man into the boards"?

Reducing the angle of your opponent's forward progress so that he is forced to skate into the boards. You then finish off your check and effectively keep him out of the play.

GOALIE STRATEGY

What is "pulling the goalie"?

Removing him from the ice and inserting a skater in his place. Then you have six skaters and the other team has only five skaters (plus its goalie).

Under what conditions would a team remove its goalie?

If the team is losing by one or two goals, it is quite commonplace for that team to "pull its goalie" in the last minute or two of the game. The purpose is to add one more skater, put a great deal of pressure on the opponents, and score a goal or two.

Why does a team pull its goalie during a delayed penalty?

There is little chance that the offending team will score because in a delayed penalty the ref blows his whistle as soon as the offending team has possession of the puck. The *non-offending* team pulls its goalie to immediately add an additional skater, even if it is for just a few seconds, in the hope of scoring a goal.

What's the best moment to pull the goalie?

Many think you should pull your goalie *during play* and hope that the other team will not observe that your goal is empty. It's important to retain control of the puck and keep it in the opponents' defending zone, and not allow them to shoot at your empty net.

How often does a team pull its goalie in the final minute if it's losing by one goal?

Almost always.

What if the team that pulls its goalie accidentally shoots the puck into its own goal? Does it count as a score?

Sadly, yes!

What's a "screen shot"?

This is a shot on goal when the goalie's vision is marred by one or several (usually opposing) players in front of him. Often on a successful screen shot, the goalie never sees the puck until it hits the net behind him. This is the most difficult shot for most goalies to stop.

During a power play, why is it advisable to shoot low line drives at the goalie?

With so many bodies on his end of the ice during the power play, the goalie is often screened and a low line drive is particularly difficult for him to see. Also, low line drives increase the number of rebounds, giving the attacking team an additional scoring chance.

FORWARDS

Who are considered to be forwards?

The center and the two wings.

Do forwards ever play defensively, or is their job to be strictly an offensive force and leave the defense to the goalie and the two defensemen?

Forwards play defensively when backchecking. The team that fails to *backcheck* effectively will almost always lose.

What special talents does a coach try to combine in a three-player forward line?

One player who is an effective stickhandler, another who is good at digging the puck out of the corners, and a third who has a blazing shot. This combination is often described as "a checker, a playmaker, and a scorer," and the three playing together are very effective.

What's a breakaway?

One of the most exciting plays in any game, a breakaway occurs when a player has the puck and there is no one between him and the goalie. "One on one," it's an excellent scoring opportunity for the skater.

Although the breakaway is exciting and dramatic, what should the offensive player always be trying to do?

Trying to set up a two-on-one situation. That means *two* of your players against only *one* defenseman.

If your teammate has the puck, what should you be trying to do?

Get clear. Position yourself alone to receive a pass so then you can either:

1. Take a shot on goal.
2. Pass the puck to a teammate who is in a better position to score than you are.

DEFENSE

What are the basic strategies while playing defense?

1. Prevent the other team from getting an opportunity to score.
2. Regain possession of the puck.

When your team "beats the defense," what have they accomplished?

They have gotten by the defensemen while on a rush at the opponent's goal, and have gotten off a shot.

If you are the lone defenseman between your goal and an opponent who has the puck, should you "go for the puck" or "go for the man"?

Go for the man and don't even look at the puck. If he stickhandles around you, he's in on your goalie all alone, and you've allowed a breakaway.

You are an NHL defenseman and you intend to block a shot on goal with your body by dropping down on one or both knees at the last minute. Why must you correctly judge how high your opponent will probably shoot the puck?

It's your intention to stop the puck with your thighs or chest. Not your face. If you think his shot might be waist level, you would want to remain on your skates and *not* drop to the ice on your knees. That's why you must quickly estimate how high he will shoot the puck. This is a difficult skill to master and to obtain this skill requires courage and a high threshold of pain.

How does a team defend itself against a "five-on-four" power play?

The four players of the defending team form a "box" inside their own defending zone. Two players position themselves inside and parallel to their own blue line at the "points." The other two players position themselves near the net, one in front of the goal and the other on the side nearest the location of the puck. The purpose of setting up this rectangular box is to keep the opposing team from taking a shot on goal from certain dangerous shooting areas like the "slot."

What's the strategy on a "five-on-four" power play when the opponents are very skillful at passing the puck? When the opponents are not so skillful?

If the opponents are skilled passers, your team will probably try to maintain a rigid box to prevent passes to the slot. Your opponents will try to shoot from the slot because it is such an advantageous location from which to shoot at your goal. If your opponent is a weak passing team, you will want to put a lot of pressure on the puck carrier and try to force him into an error so that you can regain control of the puck and break up their power play.

In a five-on-four power play, what does the defending team do when it gains control of the puck?

It shoots the puck the length of the ice to waste some time from the penalty and to relieve the pressure in their defending zone. If they are shorthanded, they will not be called for icing. However, if there is clear skating room ahead they will retain control of the puck until pressured to shoot it the length of the ice. They will retain control for two reasons: one is to waste as much time as they can, stalling until the man comes out of the penalty box. The second reason is that teams *do* score shorthanded!

What's the strategy when your team is two men short and you're confronted with a five-on-three power play?

When the puck is in your defending zone you will set up a rotating triangle. One skater will apply pressure at the points and the other two will be near the net, trying to clear away the puck when it gets near the goal. Your three players will rotate their position on the three corners of the triangle as they follow the play of the opponents.

SPECIALISTS

What is a "policeman"?

He's a big, tough player who protects his smaller teammates from the bullies on the opposing team. His job is to hit the opposing players hard and often. He can be a rough and sometimes dirty player.

What is a "shadow"?

He's the one assigned to the other team's star. His job is to prevent the star from being an effective force for his team.

What is a "penalty killer"?

A player who is adept at stealing the puck and keeping it away from the opponents while his team is playing shorthanded.

Why do they call a certain type of player a "digger"?

This player skates fast into the corners and fights hard (digs) to control the puck. If there's a race to a free puck in the corner, he tries his best to get there first. Diggers wear down the other team and create offensive opportunities.

Does a coach designate special players to play when his team has a power play or when it is shorthanded?

Yes.

What special skills do power play specialists possess?

They must be good passers, good stick handlers, have a "nose for the puck," and be able to control the puck without getting nervous. Power play skaters are usually a team's most skilled players.

What special skills do shorthanded specialists have?

They've got to be exceptional "anticipators," sensing where and to whom their opponents will next pass the puck.

TACTICS

What is "dumping" the puck?

Shooting the puck over the opponents' blue line and into his defending zone, usually in one of the corners of the rink. Then the purpose is to rush into the zone and attempt to gain control of the puck.

What is "ragging the puck"?

Passing the puck back and forth among your own teammates for the purpose of not allowing the opponents to gain control of the puck. Ragging is used frequently when a team is shorthanded and its aim is to prevent the other team from gaining control of the puck and mounting a power play attack.

What is "penalty killing"?

This is the opposite side of the power play. The purpose is to *prevent* the other team from scoring while you are shorthanded and they have a power play. A defensive strategy.

What is "centering the puck"?

Moving the puck to the "slot" area of the rink.

SUBSTITUTION—CHANGING PLAYERS "ON THE FLY"

What do players do "on the fly"?

Hockey is the only sport in which players are substituted with no stoppage of play; no whistle is needed. They change "on the fly."

What's the most dangerous time for a team to make a line change?

When the puck is in its defending zone.

When should forwards execute a line change?

Only when the puck is in their attacking zone (their opponent's defending zone).

How often does a team change its forward line?

About every 60 seconds of playing time.

Must a team change an entire line or can individual players change?

Usually the entire line changes at one time, but it is possible for individual players to change.

How does a team know when to substitute players?

A team changes players when the players on the ice are tired, generally every 45–60 seconds. Players come off the ice when they are fatigued or when the puck is in their attacking zone. Players never change when the puck is in their own defending zone or even looks like it might go into their defending zone. Making a blunder like that would leave their team outnumbered and create a very desirable scoring opportunity for the opposition.

Who gives the signal for players to substitute "on the fly"?

The coach informs the players on the bench when to relieve the tired skaters on the ice. Some coaches signal their players to return to the bench as soon as possible by whistling at them. A coach may whistle a line off the ice if he's attempting to match a specific line on his team against a specific line on the opposing team.

Why do lines change so often?

Hockey is a very fast game and for players to sustain this rapid pace they must be relieved before they are fatigued.

Does a team ever substitute five *players at once?*

Yes, but most often you'll see a front line change *or* a defensive line change, not both at once. However, in European hockey the "wholesale" change of all five players is more common.

When a team is changing lines, how close to the players bench must a departing player be before his substitute can leave the bench and join in the play?

In the NCAA, the departing player must be out of the play and within three to five feet from the bench. The NHL requires the player to be out of the play and within five feet of the bench.

MORE QUESTIONS ABOUT STRATEGY

What's a "chippy" game?

A game when both teams are very physical, with much checking and many penalties.

What is "freezing the puck"?

Deliberately holding the puck against the boards with your skates or your stick for the purpose of forcing a face-off.

Why would a team want to "freeze" the puck against the boards?

To stop the momentum if it was going against them. Play is stopped and a face-off follows.

What is "clearing the puck"?

Shooting the puck to the other end of the rink. You do this when your opponents are creating a great amount of pressure around your goal and you need to relieve that pressure. Besides, your opponents cannot possibly score if the puck is in *their* end of the rink!

What are the three basic methods for deking (faking) an opponent?

1. Drop your head, shoulders or hip one way; then move the other way.
2. Hold the stick as if you were going one way, shift your stick, and quickly move the other way.
3. Combine the above two methods in a smooth and swift action.

When, during a game, does a team usually take its 30-second time out?

Near the end of the third period.

What three main methods might a player in a face-off use to try to gain control of the puck?

1. Sweeps the puck with a backhand motion intended to pull the puck *back* to one of his own players.
2. Moves the puck *forward* to a teammate.
3. Ties up his opponent in the face-off so he cannot control the puck while a teammate rushes in and seizes the puck.

If you are up against the boards fighting for control of the puck and you believe you are going to be unsuccessful, what can you do?

Attempt to freeze the puck against the boards, forcing a face-off.

Even though a team is at full strength, when might it want to ice the puck?
1. When its defense is under heavy pressure and is disorganized.
2. When its players need a line change but can't perform it smoothly.
3. When a player is hurt.
4. When a player has broken or lost his stick.

What is the strategy with a man advantage (power play)?
1. Gain control of the puck.
2. Get the puck into the attacking zone.
3. Pass the puck back and forth rapidly trying to find your "open man." Since you have a man advantage, one of your players should be open.
4. Pass the puck to your open man, who should be in the best position to fire an effective shot on goal.
5. After the shot is taken, regain possession of the puck and begin the process of locating your open man all over again.

Q.   *Before the goalies' mask was accepted as required equipment, did a goalie often lose a tooth or two?*
A.   *Goalie John Bower of Toronto (who played from 1953 to 1970) lost 28 teeth.*

Is there a strategy in seating your players on the bench?
Yes. Seat your defending players close to your defending zone. This way, when they jump over the boards onto the ice, they are closer to their defending position by a few strides.

What are the advantages of being the home team?
1. In your home rink, you have a better knowledge of the boards and glass, how the puck bounces off them, etc.
2. The applause and support of the home crowd should lift your spirits and induce you to play your best.
3. In a face-off, the official waits until the home team player places his stick blade on the ice before he drops the puck between the two opposing players. This gives the home team player a slight advantage because he can better sense when the puck will drop.
4. Because the visiting team must submit its starting lineup before the home team does, the latter is in a better position to counter their opponent's starting lineup.

What is the "dump and chase" strategy?
It's a style of play in which one team shoots or "dumps" the puck into the opponent's end, then tries to either get to the puck first, wrest control of the puck, or force the opposing team to make a poor defensive play.

In a face-off, what does each player attempt to do?
Although the strategy varies depending upon the location of the face-off, time remaining in the game, the score, etc., each player attempts to gain control of the puck directly or put himself in a position relative to his opponent so that he can gain control of the puck as soon as possible.

When not playing on the ice, why do all the forwards on your team sit on the end of the players' bench that's closest to your team's attacking zone?
When a team decides to substitute a new forward line, the players who are on the ice at that time will first shoot the puck into their attacking zone. When the new forward line relieves the tired forward line, each of the new players will want to skate into their attacking zone where the puck is. Sitting on that end of the bench nearest their team's

attacking zone reduces the distance the new forward has to skate before he's in his attacking zone. Every second counts!

Which former team president is responsible for the now common practice of removing the goalie for an extra attacker whenever the ref calls a delayed penalty?
Weston Adams, Sr., president of the Bruins, 1964–69.

In the "old days," what was a favorite tactic of a team under pressure?
Before 1930, a team under pressure could ice the puck as many times as they wanted with no penalty. In one game the visiting New York Americans iced the puck 61 times against the Boston Bruins in a 3–2 win.

How did Bruins' owner Charles Adams react to this constant icing?
He suggested that when a team iced the puck, the puck should be brought back for a face-off, just as it happens now. But when the other NHL governors turned thumbs down on Adams' proposed rule change, he had his Bruins ice the puck 87 times in the next game against the Americans. The hockey fans booed the action (or really inaction) so loudly that the icing rule was changed to closely resemble the current icing rule.

What rule change early in the history of the NHL affects the style of play of goaltenders to this day?
In the NHA, predecessor to the NHL, goalies who fell to the ice were assessed a minor penalty. But the style of Clint Benedict of Ottawa was to sprawl on the ice. Rather than make the continual assessment of penalties a farce, the league changed the rule in 1915 to allow goaltenders from then on to sit, lie down, or sprawl any way they wished.

(Left to right) Lynn, Lester, and Patrick celebrate as the N.Y. Rangers tie the NHL record of 18 games without a defeat on January 11, 1940.
(© Bruce Bennett Studios)

Does a coach usually play his best offensive players on the same line, or does he distribute these better players among two or more lines?

It varies from coach to coach, but most put their best offensive players on the first two lines.

Do hockey players have set plays like basketball and football players do?

Yes, but you're more likely to see designed plays on face-offs, power plays, and shorthanded situations. Hockey is so fast and such a "read and react" game that it's difficult to execute formal, designed plays.

Chapter 12
ROLLER HOCKEY

When it's summertime, you still want to play hockey, but there's no ice. Try roller hockey.

BASICS

How many roller hockey players are there?
About 3.5 million people will play roller hockey this year, most of them youths.

Are there professional leagues?
Yes, and their games are often on TV.

What organized games are there for kids?
The Youth League age groups: 8 and under, 10 and under, 12 and under, 14 and under, 17 and under, 18 and over (adult).

Where is the game of roller hockey played?
Throughout the world. In the US, growth is fastest in the Sun Belt and California.

How many players on a team?
Four skaters and a goalie. Teams are limited to 17 total players including two goalies.

What type of surfaces is it played on?
Any hard flat surface, such as concrete. Outside on tennis courts, parking lots, rinks, and even driveways. Inside on roller hockey rinks.

How long is the roller hockey season?
Outdoors, it's played whenever the surface is dry.
Indoors, it's played year round.

What is the size of the rink?
The "official" size is 185' x 85' but rink size varies
depending on what is available to play on: tennis court,
parking lot, old roller skating rinks, etc.

How long is a game?
Because most indoor roller rink operators charge by the
hour, most games fit into a one-hour time frame. Typically,
there is a five-minute warm-up period before the start of
the game. When there is no visible game clock, the game is
two 15–25 minute halves (running time) with a five-minute
period between each half.
If there is a visible game clock, teams will play two
12–15-minute halves (stop time) with a five-minute rest
period between each half.

Are there "boards" around the rink?
Yes. They can range in height from 8″ to 42″.

How many zones on the rink?
There are only two zones, a team's defending zone and
its attacking zone. The rink is divided in half.

What's the average number of goals scored in a game?
Twelve. In ice hockey the average is seven.

RULES

How does a game begin?
Like ice hockey, with a face-off at center rink.

When is a player offside?
A player is never offside. There are no offside rules.

Is icing ever called?
No.

Are games allowed to end in a tie?
Regular season games can end in a tie. In tournaments, teams will play a five-minute overtime. If still tied, four players from each team will play a "shootout."

Is a team allowed to make substitutions "on the fly"?
Yes, just as in ice hockey.

Are two-line passes allowed?
Yes, since there are no blue lines and only one center line.

What is the size of the goal?
The same as ice hockey, 4' x 6'.

Regardless of penalties, what are the fewest number of skaters a team must have playing at one time?
Two. Regarding power plays, there can be four-on-three, four-on-two, and three-on-two.

Is fighting allowed?
No. Fighting is a major five-minute penalty plus suspension from the remainder of the game and the following game.

Is checking allowed?
No.

EQUIPMENT

What protective equipment do players wear?
The same equipment that ice hockey players wear but lighter in weight and affording more ventilation. All players are urged to use a helmet, full face mask, mouth guard, gloves, elbow pads, shin guards, and an athletic cup and supporter for men and a sports bra for women.

What is the cost of equipment?
From $200 to $400.

What is the skate like?
Skates have four wheels "in line," one behind the other.

What is a "rockered" skate?
A rockered skate has the first and fourth wheel slightly higher above the playing surface than the second and third wheel. This allows the player to turn faster, and make sharper turns. A rockered skate is roller hockey's answer to the arc of an ice hockey skate.

What are sticks made of?
Wood, aluminum, or graphite. They are similar to ice hockey sticks.

Where does a person buy equipment?
Department stores, sporting goods stores, toy stores, used sporting goods stores, and specialty roller hockey stores.

What is the puck made of?
Usually some type of plastic. It weighs about half as much as a rubber ice hockey puck.

Some Hockey Terms and What They Mean

AHAUS Amateur Hockey Association of the United States.

Back check When the three forwards race back to their defending zone to try to regain possession of the puck from the opposition.

Beat the defense To get by the opposing defensemen and take a shot on the goal.

Beat the goalie To score on the goalie.

Blind pass To pass the puck without looking.

Breakaway When one or two players skate in toward the goalie with no opponents between them and the goal.

Breakout When the attacking team emerges from its defending zone and begins to pass and skate up the ice toward the opponents' goal.

Boarding Checking an opposing player into the boards.

Boards This is the hard vertical surface about four feet high that surrounds the rink. On top of the boards is plexiglass.

Clear the puck Shooting the puck just to get it away from your goal.

Deke When a puck carrier stickhandles around an opponent by faking him. A deke is a fake.

Digger A very determined hockey player who relentlessly pursues the puck until he gains possession of it.

Face-off   When the official drops the puck between the sticks of two opposing players. A procedure used to start play or to resume play.

Feed the puck   To pass the puck to another player.

Floater   A forward who sneaks (legally) into the neutral zone for the purpose of receiving a pass and making a breakaway on the opposing goal. He seldom backchecks.

Forecheck   Used when the opponents have possession of the puck in their own defending zone. Forechecking is an attempt to prevent them from getting out of their defending zone while at the same time trying to steal the puck from them.

Forward   Either a left wing, center, or right wing. Each line has three forwards.

Foul   Same as a penalty.

Freeze the puck   Using a stick or a skate to pinch or hold the puck against the boards for the purpose of stopping action and causing a face-off.

Goalie   Same as goaltender.

Goalie's crease   A light-colored blue half circle with a radius of six feet in front of each goal. This is the goalie's territory. An opposing player who charges the goalie when he's within his crease will be assessed a minor or major penalty. However, the goalie is *not* "fair game" when he ventures outside his crease.

Hash marks   Lines that extend from the face-off circles. When a face-off takes place in a face-off circle, players of each team must stay on their own side of the hash mark. This helps keep players separated.

Hat trick   Scoring three goals in one game.

Lie   The degree of "erectness" of a hockey stick. The more erect it is, the greater is its lie. Some players want to carry the puck in close to them. These players would want a more erect or "upright" stick with a high lie.

NCAA   National Collegiate Athletic Association.

NHA   National Hockey Association.

NHL   National Hockey League.

On the fly   While play is underway. Players are substituted "on the fly", i.e., they enter and leave the ice while play is underway. They do not wait for time to be called.

Open ice   A part of the ice that is free of opposing players.

Penalties   Players are assessed penalties for infractions of the rules. The NHL has eight categories of penalties, the NCAA, seven.

Playmaker   The player, usually the center, who starts and plans the play his team will use to move the puck from their defending zone to the attacking zone.

Points   A location just inside the opponents' blue line where the defensemen station themselves when their team possesses the puck and the action is in the opponents' defending zone.

Power play   When a team has a one- or two-player advantage due to a penalty, it attempts to put all five of its players in the opponents' defending zone, passing the puck back and forth until it scores a goal.

Pull the goalie   In the last minute of a game in which a team is losing, the coach will often remove the goalie and replace him with a sixth skater, hoping the added pressure will help his team score.

Pure hat trick   Scoring three consecutive goals.

Rag   Keeping possession of the puck by clever stickhandling.

Rebound   A puck that caroms off the goalie's pads and lands in front of the goal mouth. Many goals are scored on rebounds.

Ref   Same as referee.

Referee's crease   This is an area on the ice in front of the penalty timekeeper's bench. Marked in red, it is a semicircle with a radius of ten feet. This is the ref's "private area" and any player who enters or remains in this area while the ref is reporting to or consulting with any game official will be assessed a misconduct penalty in both the NCAA and NHL.

Save   When a goalie stops a puck and "saves" a goal.

Scramble   When several players on both sides pounce on a loose puck trying to gain possession of it.

Screen shot   When a goalie does not have a clear view of the puck as it is shot at him because the puck is partially or totally blocked from his sight by one or more players on either team.

Shorthanded   A team that has fewer players on the ice than its opponents because one or more of its players has been penalized.

Sin bin   Another name for the penalty box.

Sixth skater   Often when a team is behind by one of two goals in the last minute or two, it pulls its goalie off the ice and substitutes another skater. Now this team has six skaters while the opponents have only five skaters.

Slot   An unmarked spot between the face-off circles in front of the goal.

Slow whistle   When an official delays blowing his whistle because the non-offending team has possession of the puck at the moment. When the offending team regains possession of the puck, he then blows his whistle.

Split the defense   When the puck carrier is able to navigate between the two defensemen and still maintain possession of the puck.

Spot pass   When a player passes the puck to a specific location on the ice, not directly to another player. Another player will then skate to that "spot," retrieve the waiting puck, and complete the play.

Trailer   This is a player who follows the puck carrier by ten or 15 feet and puts himself in position to receive a backward pass or a drop pass.

Two-on-one   When a team is fortunate to have two attacking players with the puck and only one defensive player between them and the goalie.

Wing   On every forward line, there are three players: a left wing, a center, and a right wing. The wings patrol the sides of the rink, although because of the fast changing conditions of the game they change positions continually.

Zamboni   The customized Jeep-like vehicle which makes a new ice surface before the game and between periods.

ABOUT THE AUTHOR

John Sias is a former writer for the Associated Press, a former college hockey player, and the retired owner of a public relations firm. He was a Big Brother for ten years and a foster parent for eight years. He lives in Hollis, New Hampshire.